Creative
EMBROIDERY
& QUILTING

A J.B. Fairfax Press Publication

CONTENTS

EMBROIDERY 4

Stitch Guide 6

Perfect White Plus 10
Tablecloth and Napkins
Camisole and Pants

Trousseau Treasures 16
A Voile Nightgown
Embroidered Towels
Embroidered Bed Linen

The Rose Garden 26

A Pot Pourri 28

Beautiful Blooms 30
Re-embroidered Chintz
  Cushion
The Secrets of Chintz
Silk Floral Boudoir Cushion
Cross Stitch Cushion

Embroider a Stencil 40
Stencilled Tablecloth and
  Napkins

Charming Cross Stitch 44
Monogrammed Handkerchief
Jewellery Cushion

Cornelli Wool
  Embroidery 48

Top: Silk Floral Boudoir Cushion
(page 36)

EDITORIAL
Craft Editor: Tonia Todman
Managing Editor: Judy Poulos
Editorial Consultant: Beryl Hodges
Editorial Assistant: Ella Martin
Editorial Coordinator: Margaret Kelly
Craft Assistants: Martina Oprey, Rosa Alonso,
Tina Murphy, Yvonne Deacon, Jocelyn Mitchell,
Paula McPhaill

PHOTOGRAPHY
Andrew Elton, Harm Mol

ILLUSTRATIONS
Lesley Griffith

DESIGN AND PRODUCTION
Manager: Sheridan Carter
Layout: Lulu Dougherty
Finished Art: Steve Joseph

Published by J.B. Fairfax Press Pty Limited
80-82 McLachlan Avenue
Rushcutters Bay 2011 Australia
A.C.N. 003 738 430

Formatted by J.B. Fairfax Press Pty Limited
Printed by Toppan Printing Co, Singapore

JBFP 312
CREATIVE EMBROIDERY & QUILTING
ISBN 1 86343 085 7

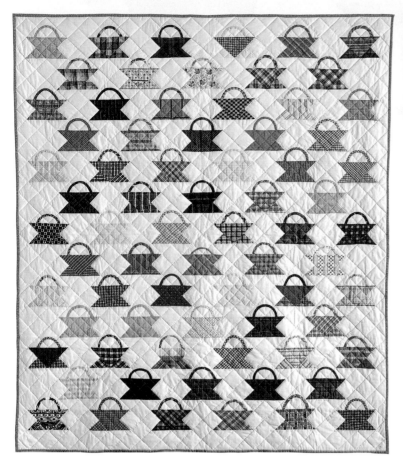

Above: Basket Quilt (page 82)
Above right: Flying Geese (page 90)

QUILTING   50

The Quilt Story   52

The Quilter's Cupboard
Material Matters
Quilting Skills
Appliqué Quilts

Metric/Imperial
Conversion Chart   63

Traditional Quilts   64

Log Cabin Quilts
Create a Quilt
Single Irish Chain
Tied Patches
Stars
Basket Quilt
Triangle Wall Quilt
Flying Geese
Garden Path
Patchwork Nursery Quilt

Templates and Designs   100

EMBROIDERY

*Today, creative stitchery is enjoying a worldwide revival. We are
fortunate to have access to an enormous variety of fabrics and threads in
hundreds of colours. Embellishing fabric with stitching has been known since before
Roman times and has been not only a popular pastime but a way of creating
something which is unique to the maker. We hope you enjoy the
delightful designs for home and family in this book.*

It is possible to embroider on just about any kind of fabric, natural or man-made, open weave or close, light or dark. Which fabric you choose will determine how your work will look.

Lightweight cottons and linens are ideal for delicate work such as shadow stitch embroidery. Heavier weight fabrics are best for the 'more casual' quicker stitches such as long and short stitch and cross stitch. Use canvas in its various weights from as little as six threads to the inch to as many as twenty-two for petit point, cross stitch and even rug-making.

Embroidery threads come in various lengths. Take care when pulling the end out of a new skein that you do not tangle it. Experiment to find the length of working thread that best suits you - generally this will be about 40 cm. Cut your skein into working lengths before you begin stitching and then store them carefully, ready for use. Use either cotton or wool for embroidery, wool being most commonly reserved for canvas work.

Stranded cotton (known as floss) is a glossy, twisted six-strand thread which is usually separated into two or three strands for finer work. Coton à broder is a single-stranded cotton, similar to pearl cotton but is finer and less shiny. It is easier for children and beginners to use. Pearl cotton is a shiny two-ply thread in three weights and is not separated. Soft embroidery cotton has no shine and being quite thick is mostly used on heavier fabrics.

Stranded pure silk is a very shiny, seven-stranded thread which comes in wonderful colours, ideal for special effects.

Crewel wool is used for delicate canvas work and Persian wool is a three-strand wool which can be divided. Tapestry wool is a tightly-twisted four-ply wool, also known as Gobelin wool, and is used for embroidery and canvas work.

There are three basic types of needles used in needlework — crewel, chenille and tapestry. All three come in a number of sizes and thicknesses. The one you choose depends on the work you are doing, the fabric and the yarn. *Crewel* are the sharp-pointed needles most commonly used in embroidery.

Chenilles are thicker and longer than crewels and are best for thicker fabric and yarns.

Tapestry needles have a blunt tip making them most suitable for canvas, tapestry and counted thread work.

An embroidery hoop or frame is a most useful tool. It helps to keep your work even without too much distortion of the fabric. Hoops keep the fabric taut between two rings and are adjustable to deal with different weights of fabric. If you are working on part of quite a large piece, the hoop will hold that part of it stretched. Frames keep the whole of the work stretched at the same time. You can make your own frame to the size of your work, simply by joining four pieces of wood into an open square of the right size and tacking your fabric over the frame. The wood is available pre-cut and ready to use.

STITCH GUIDE

BLANKET STITCH

This stitch is very useful for decorative edging. Working from left to right, bring the needle up at the lower edge and take a stitch from the upper edge back to the lower edge as shown in Fig. 1. Continue to take evenly spaced stitches in this way, keeping the thread under the needle (Fig. 2).

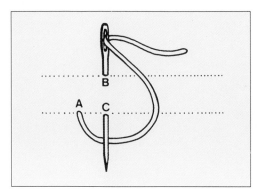

Fig. 1

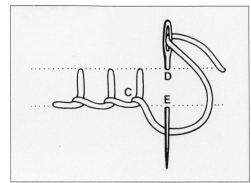

Fig. 2

BULLION STITCH ROSES

Also known as grub roses, these pretty motifs are made from an arrangement of Bullion stitches, worked in toning shades of thread from the darkest in the centre to the lightest at the edge. To make a Bullion stitch, bring the needle to the right side at A and take a stitch to B, bringing the needle up again at A (Fig. 1). Do not pull it through. The distance from A to B equals the length of the final Bullion stitch. Wind the thread around the needle, covering the length from A to B (Fig. 2). Pull the needle through, easing the twisted thread down onto the fabric. Reinsert the needle at B (Fig. 3).

To form the rose, lay down the Bullion stitches, beginning at the centre and building them up in concentric circles with each one at a slight angle to the one before.

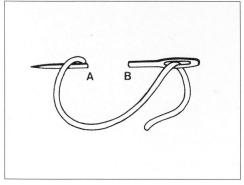

Fig. 1

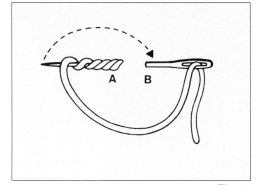

Fig. 2

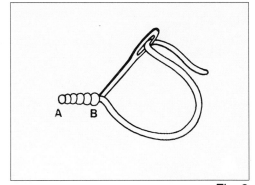

Fig. 3

RAISED BUTTONHOLE STITCH

Buttonhole stitch is worked like Blanket stitch but with the stitches very close together. Outlining the area in small running stitches will give a raised appearance (Fig. 1 and Fig. 2).

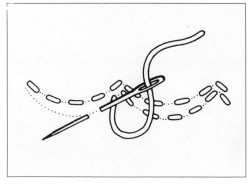

Fig. 1

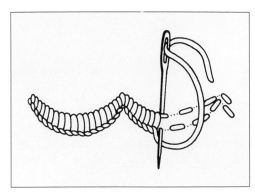

Fig. 2

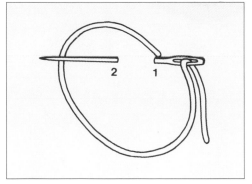

Fig. 1

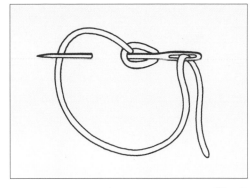

Fig. 2

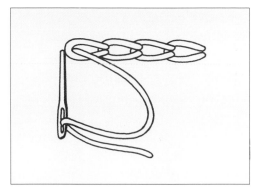

Fig. 3

CHAIN STITCH

Chain stitch is a very versatile embroidery stitch. It can be used in single rows to work a line, to outline or, with rows worked closely together, it can even fill in an area with a block of colour. Work Chain stitch as shown in Fig. 1 and Fig. 2. When the row is complete take a small stitch over the last loop of the chain to secure it as shown in Fig. 3.

CLOSE HERRINGBONE STITCH

This stitch is often used in shadow work embroidery. Working on the wrong side of the work, take a stitch at the lower left outline then take a stitch at the upper outline, bringing the needle out on the wrong side and to the left of the thread. Take a stitch back to the lower outline, bringing the needle out on the wrong side as shown in Fig. 1. Continue to work in this way, crisscrossing from left to right filling in the space required.

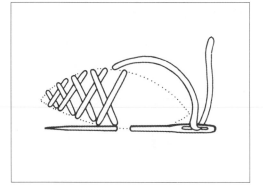

Fig. 1

CROSS STITCH

Cross stitch is the most popular embroidery stitch for almost any type of fabric, especially even-weave fabrics whose threads help you place the stitches. Cross stitch is usually worked in rows of evenly spaced stitches, where one arm of the cross is worked all across the row with the stitches all slanting in the same direction (Fig. 1), then the other arm is worked coming back the other way (Fig. 2). When you work individual Cross stitches make sure that the top arms all run in the same direction.

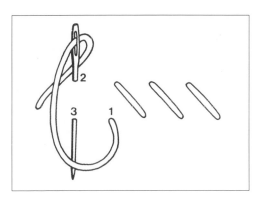

Fig. 1

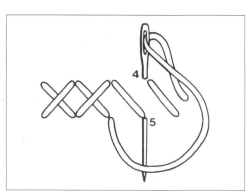

Fig. 2

EYELET STITCH

Outline the area of the eyelet with small running stitches. Make a hole in the centre with sharp scissors or a hole punch. Push the threads through to the wrong side. Working your way around the circle from left to right, stitch closely, overcasting the raw edge and the running stitches (Fig. 2).

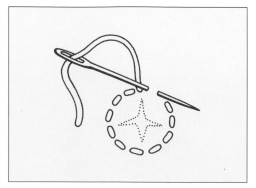

Fig. 1

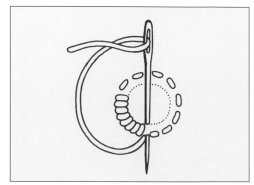

Fig. 2

FRENCH KNOTS

French Knots are ideal for flower centres. Begin the stitch by bringing the needle up through the fabric and winding the thread around it twice as shown in Fig. 1. Gently pulling the thread tight (Fig. 2), reinsert the needle near the point of exit and pull it through.

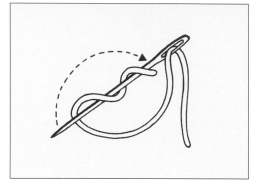

Fig. 1

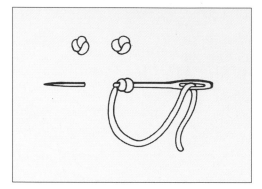

Fig. 2

HEM STITCH

Draw out the required number of threads from the fabric. Working on the wrong side make small Backstitches to secure thread and then pass the needle from right to left under the required number of threads. (See Fig. 1). Take a small vertical stitch to the right of the thread bundle into the fabric. (See Fig. 2).

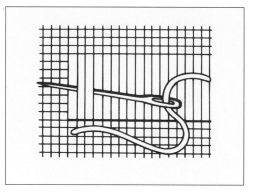

Fig. 1

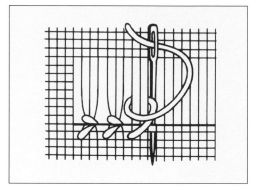

Fig. 2

LAZY DAISY STITCH

Lazy daisy stitch is popular for working flowers. It is like the last chain of a row of Chain stitch. One stitch gives the impression of a flower petal and groups are usually worked in a circle to look like a flower, as the name implies (see Fig. 1, Fig. 2).

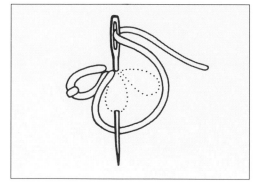

Fig. 1

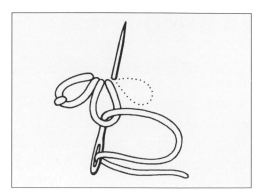

Fig. 2

LONG AND SHORT STITCH

This stitch (Fig. 1) is often used to fill in areas of colour with a slightly more textured effect than Satin stitch. You can shade colours with this stitch by stitching one set of Long and Short stitches in one colour and the next set in a slightly lighter or darker shade, blending them in quite smoothly.

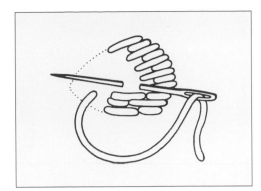

Fig. 1

OVERCAST STITCH

Use running stitch to outline the design then work Overcast stitches as shown in Fig. 1, very close together, covering the running stitches.

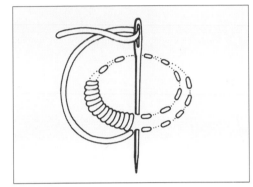

Fig. 1

RAISED SATIN STITCH

This stitch is used to give a slightly padded look to embroidery. Using small running stitches, outline and fill in the area to be covered (Fig. 1). Beginning just outside the outlining stitches and working from left to right for horizontal stitches (top to bottom for vertical stitches), work stitches close together as shown in Fig. 2.

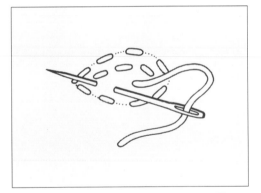

Fig. 1

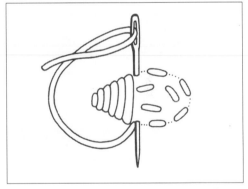

Fig. 2

STEM STITCH

This is mainly an outlining stitch which as its name implies is often used to work the stems on floral motifs. Simply work a Long stitch then come up again half a stitch back as in Fig. 1, keeping the thread below the needle. Repeat as shown in Fig. 2.

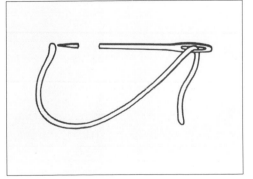

Fig. 1

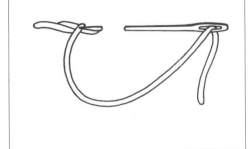

Fig. 2

Perfect
White Plus

The colour of innocence and purity: white is the perfect choice for elegant linen and exquisite underwear. The delightful floral motif we have chosen makes this charming embroidered tablecloth and matching napkins very special. Sheer cotton organdie is perfect for the delicate shadow work while the clear outlines of neatly mitred corners add a classic edge to this heirloom for tomorrow. The same techniques are also used to decorate the delicate camisole and pants.

Tablecloth and Napkins

Naturally, you can choose any size you wish for your tablecloth, but in practical terms the size will be limited by the width of the fabric. If you must join lengths of fabric to achieve the width you desire, then take care to place the seams at the table edge and not down the centre of the cloth.

MATERIALS

a square of cotton organdie, the
*   size of your choice*
45 cm squares of organdie for each
*   napkin*
sewing thread
stranded embroidery threads in the
*   following DMC colours:*
*   986 (dark green) and white*
a suitable needle
tracing paper and pencil
dressmakers carbon paper
a stylus

METHOD

See the embroidery motifs on page 100.
The same basic method is used to make the tablecloth and the napkins.

1 *To prepare your square:* Straighten all the edges of your square of organdie and cut away the selvages. Make sure that the edges follow the grain of the fabric and are not on the bias. Press in 1 cm hems all around the edges. Press in the true hemline 4 cm away from the pressed edge.

2 *To mitre the corner:* Fold the corner to the wrong side as shown in Fig. 1, making sure the pressed lines are aligned. Press. Repeat this for each corner. Open out the corners and fold the whole square

of fabric in half diagonally, with right sides together and pressed edges even. Stitch along the pressed line as shown in Fig. 2. Trim the fabric at the point and press the seam open as shown in Fig. 3. Turn the corner to the right side. Repeat this for all four corners. Press the corners and hems carefully. Stitch hems into place.

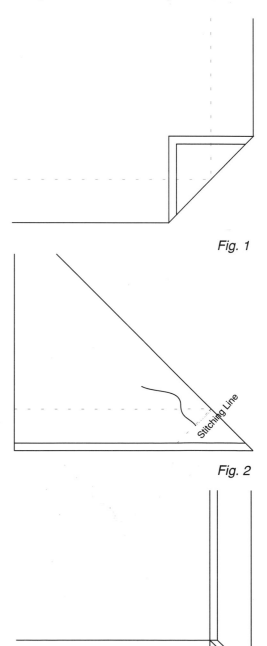

Fig. 1

Fig. 2

Fig. 3

STITCHES USED
Close Herringbone stitch for the shadow work leaves; Satin stitch for the flowers; Stem stitch for the stems

3 *For the embroidery:* Locate the floral motif on page 100 you wish to use. Trace the designs. Transfer the designs into place on the tablecloth using the dressmakers carbon paper and stylus. Embroider the leaves, stems and flowers in shadow work, using two strands of embroidery thread and following our Stitch Guide and illustrations at the front of the book. Press the tablecloth and napkins carefully.

Above: Delicate shadow work lilies of the valley decorate this organdie tablecloth and matching napkins
Left: Mitred corners give a professional finish

CAMISOLE AND PANTS

Delicate underwear is the perfect foil for shadow work embroidery but keep it simple. These bows are the perfect choice.

Use a commercial pattern for a bias-cut camisole and pants, applying the lace edge and the embroidery as instructed below.

MATERIALS

1.6 m of 115 cm wide cotton voile
4.5 m of double-edged lace for
    trimming
commercial pattern for a camisole
    and pants
tracing paper
pencil
dressmakers carbon paper
stylus
sewing thread
stranded embroidery thread in DMC
    798 (mid-blue) or the colour
    of your choice
embroidery needle
elastic

METHOD

See the embroidery motifs on page 101.

1 *For cutting out:* Cut out the pattern pieces from your fabric using your pattern, noting that they are cut on the bias of the fabric.

2 *For the embroidery:* Trace the motif designs from page 101. Transfer the designs into place on the Camisole and Pants using the dressmakers carbon paper and stylus. Embroider the bows in shadow work, following the directions for Close Herringbone stitch and Overcast stitch in the Stitch Guide at the front of the book. Take care not to distort the fabric while you are embroidering – a frame will help you with this.

3 *For the sewing:* Make all seams French seams or normal seams, trimming the seam allowances to 6 mm, then neatening them with zigzag stitching or overlocking. Place the front and back camisole pieces together with raw edges even. Stitch the side seams. Place the front and back pants pieces together at the inside legs with raw edges even. Stitch the inside leg seams. Prepare and stitch the crotch seam in the same way, stitching from the front waist through the crotch to the back waist.

4 *For the elastic:* Turn 6 mm at the waist edge to the wrong side to neaten, then turn again 1.5 cm. Stitch all around to form a casing for the elastic, leaving a gap for inserting elastic. Insert the elastic, try on the pants and adjust the elastic for comfort. Overlap the ends and stitch together. Close the gap in the casing by hand.

5 *For the lace:* Attach lace to the camisole's upper and lower edges, and the leg edges of the pants in the following way. Position the lace so that approximately $7/8$ of the lace sits on the fabric and $1/8$ is over the edge. Where necessary fold the lace into mitres or angles that will allow it to follow the fabric shape. Set your sewing machine stitch controls to a narrow zigzag stitch that is almost a Satin stitch. Stitch around the pattern of the lace close to the inner edge. Trim away the voile from underneath the lace and the excess lace inside the stitching on the right side. Oversew any angles or mitres that need to be secured, using a narrow zigzag stitch.

Top left: The shadow work bow seen from the right side
Above left: The same bow viewed from the wrong side
Above: The camisole and pants with lace trim and embroidered bows

6 *For the straps:* Measure the length for your shoulder straps and cut two pieces of bias fabric this length plus 3 cm x 2 cm. Fold the straps over double with right sides together and long edges matching. Stitch twice for strength along the long side. Turn the straps to the right side. Pin the straps in place on the front and back of the camisole so that the raw ends of the straps are tucked underneath, out of sight. Try on the camisole to adjust the strap length then handsew the ends into place.

To turn rouleau straps if you don't own a gadget made specially for the purpose, thread a large darning needle with a strong, double thread. Stitch securely at one end of the rouleau, then pass the needle down the length and out the other end. Pulling gently on the double thread, turn the rouleau to the right side.

15

Trousseau Treasures

*Not so long ago, young girls
began preparing and putting
aside beautiful bed linen and towels
for a 'hope chest' or 'glory box'.
These days, although the pace of life
seems to have overtaken
this charming old tradition,
hand-embroidered treasures like
these still delight the bride-to-be.*

*Clockwise from the left: The voile nightgown; cushion;
embroidered sheets and pillowcases; Bullion stitch rose
embroidered towels and Cross stitch embroidered towels*

A VOILE NIGHTGOWN

A soft, pure cotton, voile nightgown that's been embroidered with loving care would be a delightful addition to any trousseau. This simple style has been trimmed with lace and shadow work bows, and scattered with Bullion stitch roses.

Use a commercial pattern for the nightgown, applying the lace and embroidery as instructed below.

MATERIALS
2.7 m of 115 cm wide cotton voile
2.5 m of good quality bias binding (either cotton or satin)
2.5 m of very fine piping cord
2.5 m of 1 cm wide white satin ribbon for facing
2 m of ribbon in the same colour as the shadow work embroidery for the bow
4 m of 7 cm wide lace for the bodice and hem trim
stranded embroidery threads in the colours of your choice or DMC colours 793 (dark blue), 794 (light blue), 988 (green) and white
matching sewing thread
a suitable embroidery needle
tracing paper
pencil
dressmakers carbon paper
stylus

METHOD
See the embroidery motif on page 21.

1 *For cutting out:* Cut out the nightgown front and back pattern pieces. Cut approximately 2 m of 3 cm wide bias strips from the fabric for shoulder straps.

2 *For the embroidery:* Trace the motif from page 21, then transfer the design onto the centre front of the nightgown, using the dressmakers carbon and stylus. Embroider the motif using two strands of embroidery thread in Close Herringbone stitch, French Knots and the Bullion stitch roses as instructed in the Stitch Guide

at the front of the book. Embroider the roses around the bow.

3 *For the lace and piping:* Gather the lace just enough to cause it to stand away from the fabric when applied. Press open the bias binding and then fold it over double, with wrong sides together. Using the zipper foot of your sewing machine, stitch the piping cord into the fold of the bias binding.

4 *For the sewing:* Join the front to the back nightgown at the side seams using narrow French seams or a normal seam with the allowance stitched together 6 mm from the seam, trimmed back close to the stitching and overcast. Be sure to leave one side seam open for up to 30 cm from hem for a split.

5 *For the lace:* With the wrong side of the lace facing the right side of the nightgown and raw edges matching, baste the lace around the hem and around the side split. Make small pleats if necessary to ease the lace around the corners and curves. Gradually ease the lace away to nothing at the top of the split so that it looks as if it disappears into the top of the split. Using a fine zigzag stitch and sewing 6 mm in from the edge, stitch the lace around the hem and side split. Trim away the seam allowances close to the stitching. Starting at a side seam, baste the lace around the upper bodice in the same way as for the hem.

6 *For the piping:* Pin and baste the piping on top of the lace at the upper bodice, with raw edges

matching. Tuck the raw end of the piping under at the overlap. Stitch the piping in place using the zipper foot and with the sewing machine needle nearer to the cord or on top of the previous piping stitching. Clip the seam allowances where necessary for ease. Press the seam to the inside.

7 *For the shoulder straps:* Fold the bias strips of fabric in half lengthways with right sides together and raw edges even. Stitch down the long side, trim the seam and turn the straps to the right side. Try on the nightgown to adjust the length of the shoulder straps. Using two lengths of rouleau for each shoulder, fold each length in half and loop one through the other in the middle, so that the loop sits on the shoulder and the raw ends are at the front and the back. Handsew the raw ends in place. On the inside, handsew the 1 cm wide ribbon over the seam allowance with the top edge of the ribbon on the piping stitching, pleating the ribbon where necessary around

the angles and covering the ends of the shoulder straps. Make two thread loops on the side seams at waist level, or just above, to hold the ribbon.

To turn rouleau straps if you don't own a gadget made specially for the purpose, thread a large darning needle with a strong, double thread. Stitch securely at one end of the rouleau, then pass the needle down through the length and out the other end. Pulling gently on the double thread, turn the rouleau to the right side.

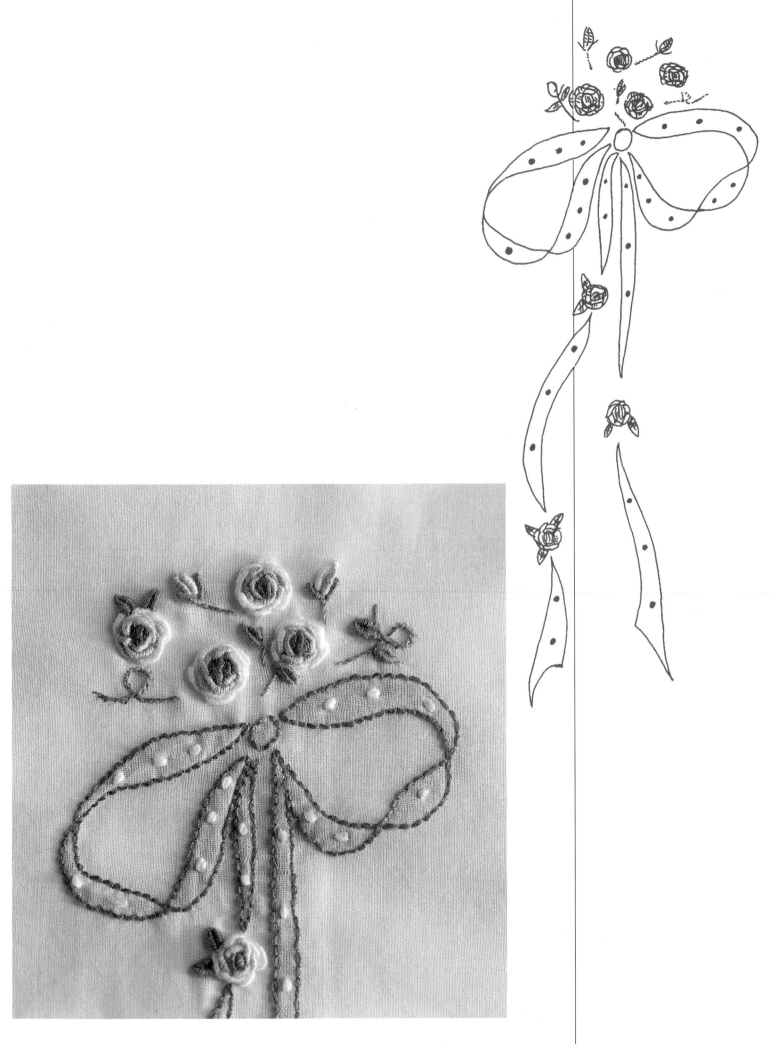

EMBROIDERED TOWELS

You can buy towels with the even-weave fabric panel already included and ready to be embroidered. If you can't buy them where you shop, you can find an even-weave band (known as Aida) at craft shops, for you to embroider then sew onto the towel when you've completed your stitching. Either way, these charming confections of ribbons, roses, rabbits and hearts should grace any bathroom.

MATERIALS

a suitable towel with or without an
even-weave band
an even-weave band to embroider
stranded embroidery threads in colours
of your choice. We used DMC
colours 3354, 10 and 800
a suitable embroidery needle

METHOD

See the embroidery design graphs on page 103.

1 *For the Cross stitch towel:* Find the centre of the band to be embroidered by folding or measuring. Sew lines of loose running stitch along the folds. The intersection of these lines marks the centre point which corresponds with the centre of the design. To find the centre of the design, join the arrows at each side with a ruler. The point where they intersect is the centre.

2 Each square on the design graph represents one cross stitch and the symbol indicates the colour to be used in the embroidery. Cross stitch the motifs following the Stitch Guide at the front of the book, counting the threads

and using the design graph as a guide for your stitches. Do not pull the threads too tightly and make sure you begin and end by running the needle through the back of a few stitches to secure the ends.

3 If you are using an even-weave band, turn under the raw ends and machine stitch the band in place across the towel.

For the Bullion stitch rose towels: Stitch sprays of Bullion stitch roses, following the Stitch Guide at the front of the book and the Rose Garden on pages 26-27. Trim with bands of lace and ribbon or satin ribbon-trimmed grosgrain as shown. Tie the ribbon into a bow and secure with small stitches.

Stitch the Bullion stitch rose towels in DMC colours: cream (746); yellow (727 and 726); pink (963, 962 and 961); peach (754, 353 and 352) and green (368 and 320).

STITCHES USED
Cross stitch for the rabbits and hearts; Bullion stitch roses and leaves

Embroidered Bed Linen

There is nothing like the feeling of slipping between crisp cotton sheets. These ones have an heirloom quality in their pretty embroidery. Trim the bed linen with colours that accent your bedroom scheme and add some beautiful cotton lace for that final touch.

MATERIALS

purchased cotton pillowcases and one flat cotton sheet
stranded embroidery threads in colours of your choice. We used DMC colours 783, 445, 307 and 444
12 cm wide cotton, single-edged lace
12 mm wide satin ribbon
a suitable embroidery needle
tracing paper
dressmakers carbon paper
pencil
stylus

METHOD

See the embroidery designs on pages 102 and 112.

PILLOWCASE

1 *For the ribbon and lace:* Pin the lace around the pillowcase opening, so that the lacy edge just overhangs the opening, beginning and ending at a side seam. Take care not to catch the flap. Open the stitching at that point for 12 cm to allow the raw ends of the lace to be pushed through. Stitch the lace in place. Pin and stitch the ribbon so that it covers the raw edge of the lace, pushing its ends through the gap. Stitch the gap closed.

2 *For the design:* Mark the centre of the lace on top of the pillowcase by measuring or folding it in half. Locate the monogram letters on page 112 and the floral designs on page 102. Trace the designs and then transfer them onto the centre of the lace.

3 *For the embroidery:* Embroider the motifs using two strands of thread and following the Stitch Guide at the front of the book. Press.

SHEETS

Follow steps 1, 2 and 3 in the Method, omitting the instructions relating to the opening of the side seams of the pillowcase.

THE ROSE GARDEN

Bullion stitch roses are a charming embroidery motif for delicate lingerie, bath towels, sleep wear or bed linen. The arrangement of the roses need only be limited by your imagination. Here are a few ideas to inspire you. Note that you can combine Bullion stitch roses with many other embroidery stitches, such as the French Knots indicated here by circles, to give the effect you are looking for. On the next page you will see how designs like these have been applied in actual embroidery.

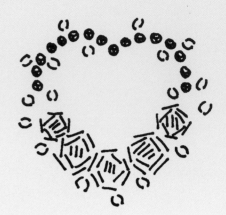

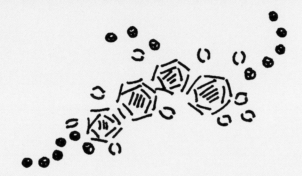

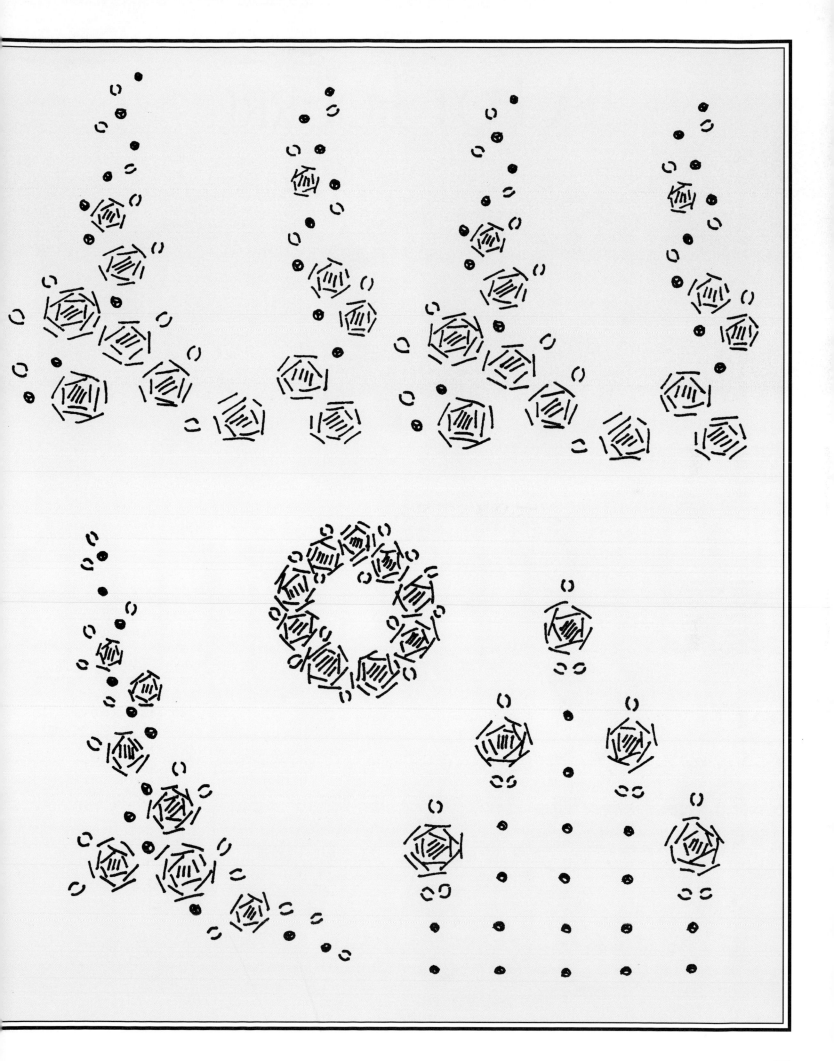

A Pot Pourri

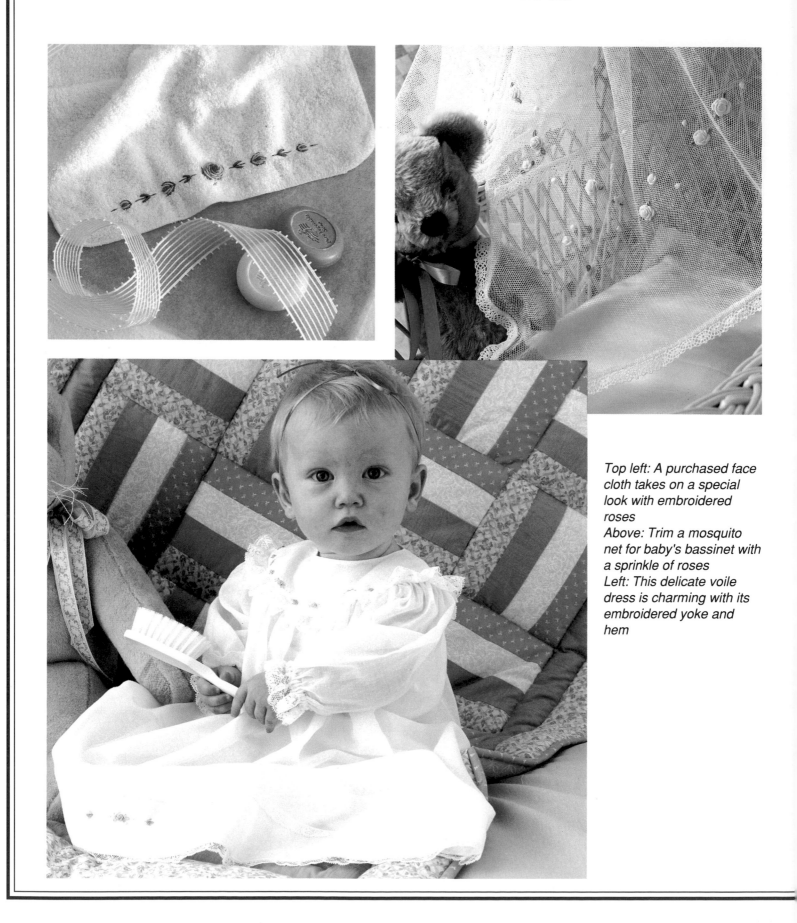

Top left: A purchased face cloth takes on a special look with embroidered roses

Above: Trim a mosquito net for baby's bassinet with a sprinkle of roses

Left: This delicate voile dress is charming with its embroidered yoke and hem

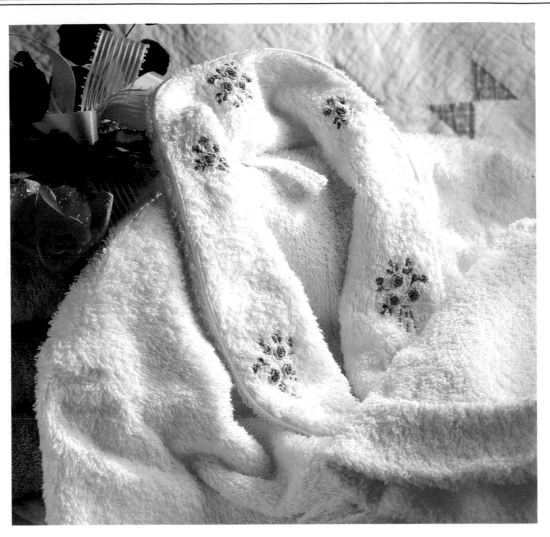

Right: Pretty as well as practical, this bathrobe is a touch of luxury

Below right: For the bride and groom on their wedding day, embroider a cover for their wedding photo album

Below: Dainty Bullion stitch roses are the perfect finishing touch for these lingerie bags

Beautiful Blooms

Embroiderers everywhere are fascinated with flowers and floral shapes. Flowers are the single most frequently recurring motif in embroidery designs. But it's only natural that, as embroiderers love beauty in all forms, they will want to reflect nature's beauty in their stitches. Pretty cushion projects will show you how to bring beautiful blooms indoors with some delightfully simple stitching.

RE-EMBROIDERED CHINTZ CUSHION

This cushion is shaped to suit the motif. We have used fabrics and colours to trim the ruffle that complements the chintz. Make your cushion in the one fabric, big or small, or with a simple contrasting piping if you prefer. Whichever method you choose you are sure to have some very original floral embroideries.

STITCHES USED

Chain Stitch for the stem and vein lines; Long and Short stitch for the petals and leaves

STITCHES

The design of your fabric will suggest the best stitches to use in embroidering. Generally, the stems and fine vein lines are best worked in tiny Chain stitches – either in lines, or in curled 'snail shell' circles to fill in the larger areas. Work petals and other broad areas of colour in Long and Short stitch. This gives you the opportunity to subtly vary the tones of colour, by shading them across the area. French knots are ideal for small dots, or even for filling in the centre of a flower, as the texture from grouped French knots is very attractive. Stem stitch, Back stitch and Satin stitch are also worth considering, and simple Blanket stitch is effective for outlining a flower.

All these stitches are outlined in the Stitch Guide at the front of the book. Work with an embroidery hoop to make your stitching easier and to prevent distortion of the fabric. Try to match closely the colour of the embroidery thread to the colour of your motif – the purpose of this type of embroidery is to embellish and add texture to the design, not to draw attention to any particular stitch.

MATERIALS

sufficient chintz fabric for the cushion front, border, cushion back and frill
sufficient contrasting fabric for the frill
sufficient 2.5 cm wide toning bias binding to go around the embroidered panel
stranded embroidery cotton in the colours of your choice
matching sewing thread
zipper
a cushion insert (purchased cushion insert or one made to measure)

METHOD

Make your cushion any size and shape that complements your fabric. Remember, your embroidered panel will be about 9 cm smaller than the finished cushion.

1 Re-embroider the centre panel of your cushion in the stitches described at left. When the embroidery is complete, turn under the outside edges of the panel and press.

2 Press open sufficient 2.5 cm wide toning bias binding. Fold it over double lengthways with right sides together. Press. Pin this bias binding under the edge of the embroidered panel so that the folded edge just protrudes. Overlap the two raw ends and then tuck them neatly out of sight under the embroidered panel. Baste.

3 Cut a piece of fabric the same shape as the embroidered panel but about 10 cm larger all around.

Place the embroidered panel onto the centre of the larger piece, taking care that the border is the same size all around. Stitch through all thicknesses around the embroidered panel.

4 Measure around the edge of the cushion front and cut two and a half times this amount of 10 cm wide fabric for the frill. Cut another identical length 12 cm wide from a contrasting fabric. Join these two strips together along one long edge with right sides facing. Join the short ends, with right sides together, to form a continuous circle. Fold the circular strip over double with wrong sides together so that the raw edges are even and press. You should have a band of contrasting fabric at the outer edge of your frill strip. If your cushion is square, mark the frill strip into quarters. Gather up the frill, starting and stopping your gathering thread at the quarter points. Pin the frill to the right side of the cushion front, placing the quarter points to the corners of the cushion front and having the raw edges even. Adjust the gathers to fit. If your cushion is oblong, mark half-way points along the long sides of the cushion front and mark the frill into two parts. Gather the frill, starting and stopping your gathering thread at the halfway points. Pin the frill around the right side of the cushion front, matching these two points and having the raw edges even. Adjust the gathers to fit.

5 Cut two back pieces, each one the same length as the front but half the width plus 3 cm. Join these pieces in a 3 cm seam, leaving an opening in the centre for the zipper. Insert zipper and leave it open.

6 Fold the frill towards the centre of the embroidered panel. Place the cushion back over the frilled front

panel with right sides facing and raw edges matching. Stitch around the outside edge, following the stitching line for the frill and taking care not to catch the frill as you sew. Turn the cushion to the right side through the zipper opening.

If a commercial cushion insert is not available in a size to suit your cushion, make a calico bag the size of your cushion leaving an opening to insert polyester fibre stuffing or feathers. Once the cushion insert is filled, handsew the opening closed.

THE SECRETS OF CHINTZ

Pretty flowered chintz, so evocative of charming country cottages and summer gardens, is widely regarded as being traditionally and thoroughly English. But chintz has a secret. It is true that chintz is traditional in England, but it is also traditional in Holland where it is called *sits* and in France where it is sometimes referred to as *indiennes* and that is where the secret lies. Yes, chintz originally came from India. The word 'chintz' is a corruption of a Hindi word *chint* or *chinta* meaning 'variegated' or 'spotted all over'. The chints, as they were originally called, were taken to Europe in the 1600s by the various East India companies, English, Dutch and French traders. They were a secondary import as the companies had gone to the East primarily to buy spices but found that Indian textiles, mainly cottons of all types, were part of the deal.

In England, the chints were tried only tentatively on the market, but soon took on and ultimately became the rage. For the first time people had lightweight cotton cloth that could be easily washed. Not only were the pretty patterns attractive but were printed in dyes that were fast. This was a miracle at the time. Europe had never known fast dyes before. Indian dyers had known how to dye cotton fast since ancient times and could produce more than one hundred colours and shades by their age-old methods. Another advantage was that the prices were low, so a large section of the population could afford them. The demand grew and by the mid-1600s the English company had imported well over a quarter of a million pieces. Everybody wanted chints!

There was the same craze in Holland where chintz was being used for clothing; and in France where *indiennes* or *toile peintes* became the rage for fashionable clothing and for furnishing. The best Indian chintz was painted and resist dyed by a slow and tedious process called *kalamkari* (literally 'penwork'); but to speed up the output to meet the huge European demand block-printing, another old Indian method, was also used. Much admired among the painted clothes were the one-off palampores (from *papangposh* meaning literally 'bedcover'). Many of these featured the 'Tree of Life' design, exotically embellished with luscious fruit, strange birds and animals in glowing colours. These became collectors' items and embroiderers loved to copy them. Embroidery was very popular in England at that time, with bedhangings and covers done in silks or in crewel wool work in flowing designs of English flowers and twining branches. Indian chintz, not dissimilar in design, was now being used.

Indian chintz and other cottons of all types continued to go to Europe for nearly two hundred years until Lancashire mastered cotton spinning and weaving. European textile printers, having found out the secrets of Indian cotton dyeing, were able to produce good copies of Indian chintz. Design differences began to develop in various countries, with English and French chintzes, for instance, gradually evolving into distinctive styles.

Chintz also travelled to faraway colonies such as Australia where Indian cottons of all types, including chintz, were imported.

In modern chintzes, Indian design influences can still be seen – watch out for stylised flowers, birds and paisley shapes that all reflect their Indian heritage.

Joyce Burnard is a journalist. She founded Ascraft fabrics, a firm which has specialised in importing Indian hand-loomed cotton into Australia. She has just completed a book which traces the fascinating connection of chintz and other Indian textiles with the West.

The chintzes on the opposite page were provided by Ascraft Fabric, Sydney

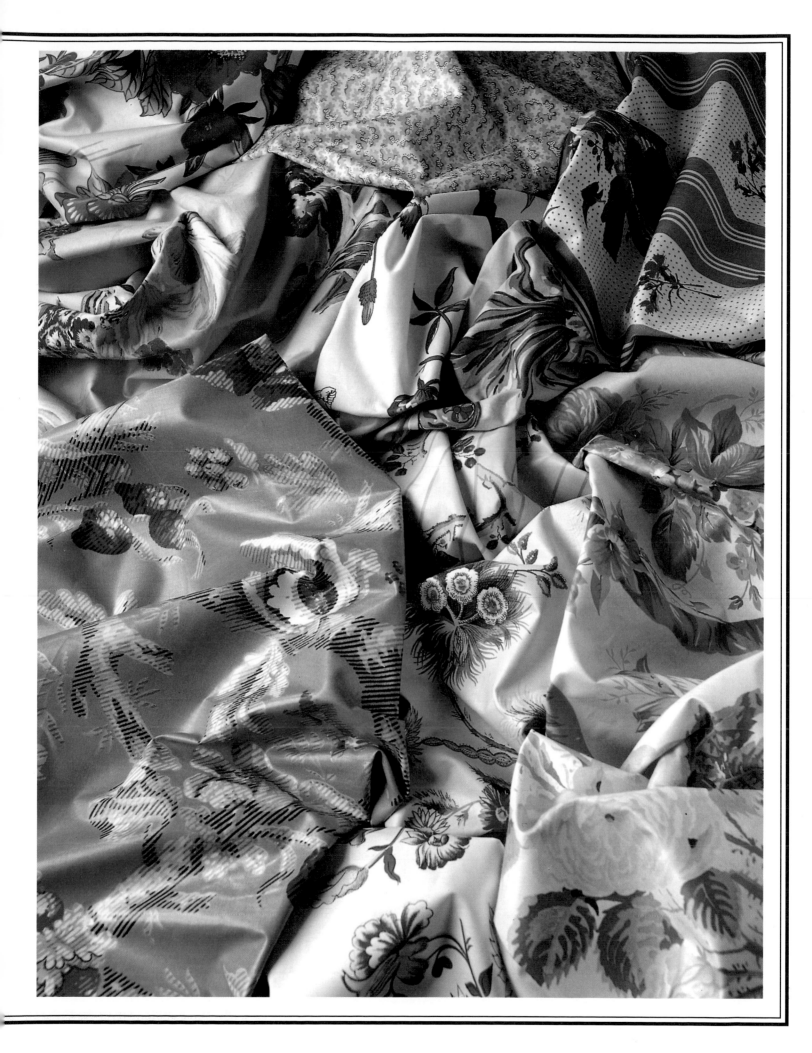

SILK FLORAL
BOUDOIR CUSHION

This charming small cushion can be made from a remnant of lovely silk. Covered with small sprays of flowers, it is embroidered in simple, tiny stitches. Our cushion measures 25 cm x 25 cm but you could expand this size and simply repeat the embroidery motifs to fill the larger area. The lace is stitched on by hand.

STITCHES USED

Bullion stitch for the roses; Lazy Daisy stitch for the daisies; Satin stitch for petals and leaves; French Knots for the dots; Stem stitch for the stems

MATERIALS

two pieces of silk for the back and front of the cushion
silk embroidery threads in the colours of your choice
sufficient 6 cm wide lace
matching sewing thread
cushion insert to fit
a suitable embroidery needle
tracing paper
pencil
dressmakers carbon paper
stylus

METHOD

See the designs on page 108.

1 *For the embroidery:* Trace the floral motifs and then transfer them onto one piece of silk, using the dressmakers carbon and stylus. Embroider the flowers, following the Stitch Guide at the front of the book.

2 *For the sewing:* Place the cushion front and back together with right sides facing and raw edges even. Stitch around the edge, leaving an opening for turning. Turn cushion right side out. Place the cushion insert inside and close the opening by hand.

3 *To finish off:* Sew the lace around the cushion by aligning the straight edge of the lace with the cushion seam and taking small stitches every 6 mm along the cushion edge, pushing the lace into folds between the stitches. Overlap and neaten the ends of the lace.

Cross Stitch Cushion

To make this pretty cushion, match the colours of your embroidery to a favourite fine cotton print – perhaps to an existing fabric in your home. There is wonderful scope here for a truly unique approach to embroidery.

MATERIALS

36 cm square of white hardanger fabric with 22 threads to 2.5 cm
stranded embroidery thread in your chosen colours. We used the DMC colours as indicated on the graph
2.1 m medium piping cord
2.1 m toning 2.5 cm wide bias binding
2.2 m of 90 cm wide fine cotton
50 cm cushion pad or insert
matching sewing thread
40 cm zipper
a suitable embroidery needle

METHOD

1 *For cutting out:* Cut four strips of fabric each 12 cm x 50 cm for the cushion border. Cut 5 m of 20 cm wide fabric for the frill. Join

pieces if necessary to achieve the desired length and two pieces 50 cm x 28 cm for the cushion back.

2 *For the embroidery:* Working with an embroidery hoop, embroider the hardanger panel following the graph and stitch key. On each side, draw out three threads 6 cm from the edge and Hem stitch along the row of holes, following the Stitch Guide at the front of the book.

3 *For the border:* Cut the ends of the border strips in perfect diagonals and join them into an open square, stopping the stitching 1 cm from the inner edge of each corner. Press under 1 cm on the inner edge of the border. Pin and baste this border evenly around the edge of the embroidered panel. Stitch along the pressed edge through all thicknesses.

4 *For the piping:* Open out the bias binding and press it flat. Fold it over double, lengthways. Insert piping cord into the fold and stitch it in place, using the zipper foot of your sewing machine. Baste this piping around the edge of the right side of the cushion front, clipping into the corners for ease.

5 *For the frill:* Join the frill strips into one continuous circle. Press it over double with wrong sides together and raw edges even. Divide and mark the circle into quarters with pins. Gather around the circle, starting and finishing at the quarter points. Pin the frill to right side corners of the cushion front, matching quarter points and with raw edges even. Adjust the

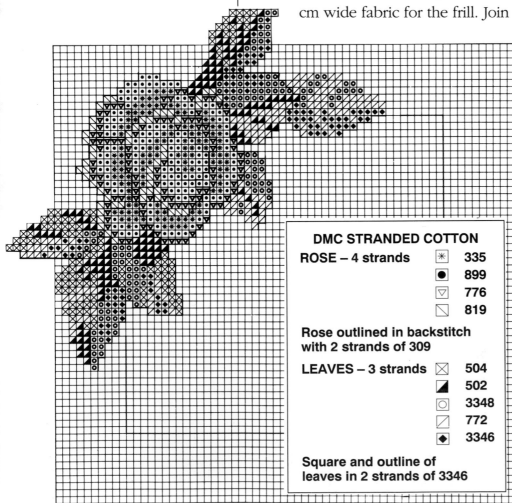

DMC STRANDED COTTON

ROSE – 4 strands

✳	335
●	899
▽	776
◺	819

Rose outlined in backstitch with 2 strands of 309

LEAVES – 3 strands

⊠	504
◪	502
○	3348
◿	772
◆	3346

Square and outline of leaves in 2 strands of 3346

gathers to fit. Stitch the frill in place, taking care not to stitch through the piping cord.

6 *For the cushion back:* Stitch the back sections together along the 50 cm edge, using a 3 cm seam allowance, and leaving a 40 cm gap for the zipper at the centre of the seam. Press the seam open and insert the zipper.

Leave the zipper open.

7 *To assemble the cushion:* Fold the frill towards the centre of the embroidered panel. Place back and front together with right sides facing and raw edges even. Stitch around the edge following the previous stitching. Turn the cushion right side out through the zipper opening.

Embroider a Stencil

Hand appliqué has always looked exquisite because it is so detailed and intricate. This can be an obstacle, preventing beginners taking up this pleasing embroidery. Here is the answer! This lovely cloth has been stencilled and re-embroidered to give the same textured effect.

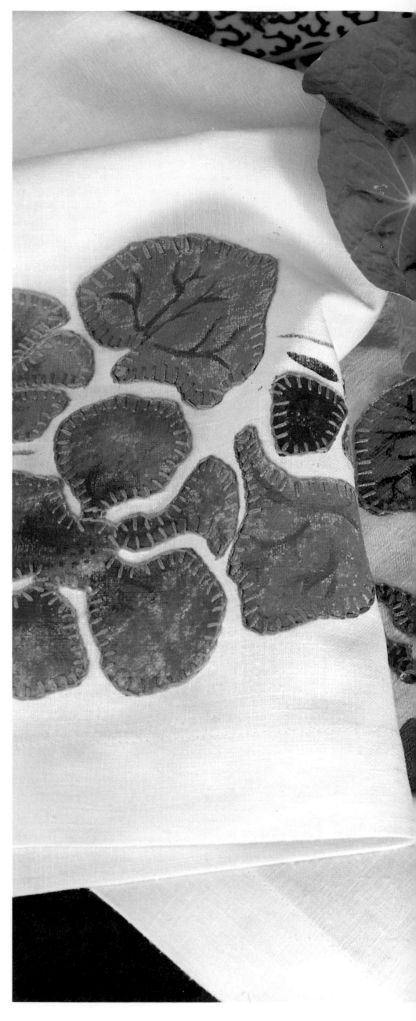

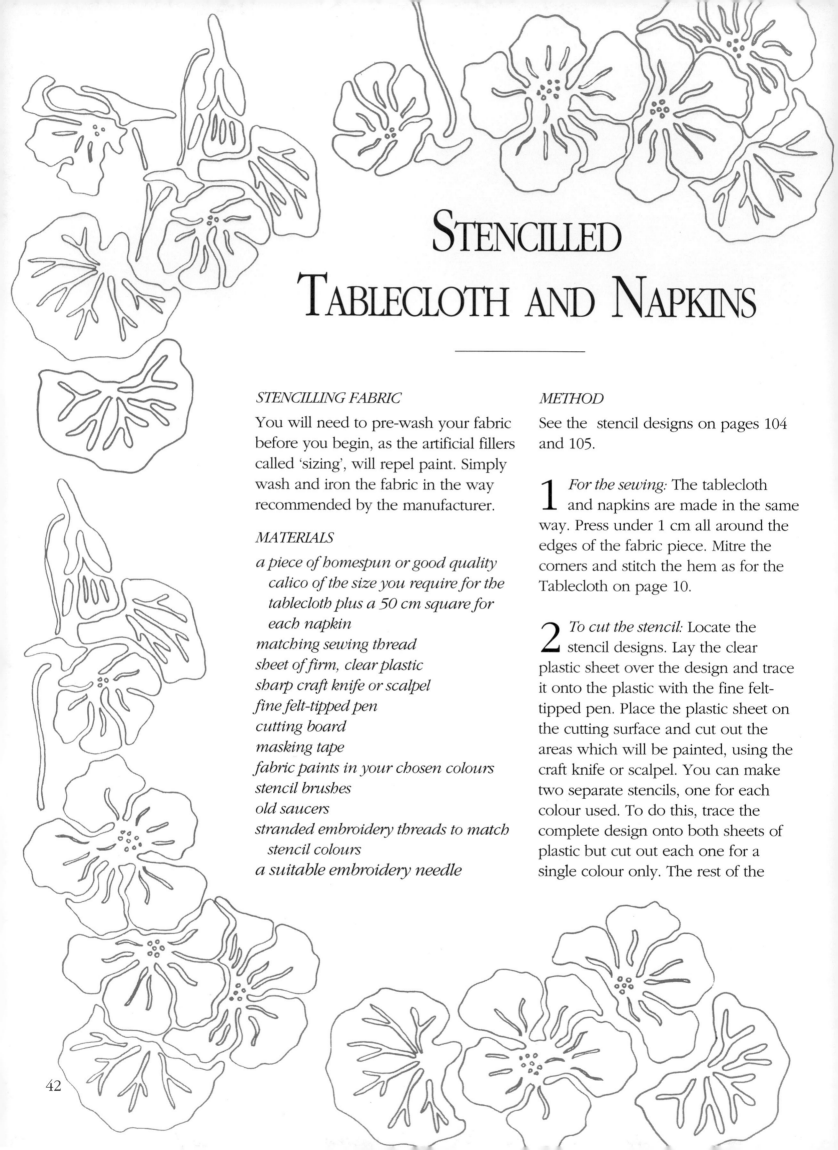

STENCILLED
TABLECLOTH AND NAPKINS

STENCILLING FABRIC

You will need to pre-wash your fabric before you begin, as the artificial fillers called 'sizing', will repel paint. Simply wash and iron the fabric in the way recommended by the manufacturer.

MATERIALS

a piece of homespun or good quality calico of the size you require for the tablecloth plus a 50 cm square for each napkin
matching sewing thread
sheet of firm, clear plastic
sharp craft knife or scalpel
fine felt-tipped pen
cutting board
masking tape
fabric paints in your chosen colours
stencil brushes
old saucers
stranded embroidery threads to match stencil colours
a suitable embroidery needle

METHOD

See the stencil designs on pages 104 and 105.

1 *For the sewing:* The tablecloth and napkins are made in the same way. Press under 1 cm all around the edges of the fabric piece. Mitre the corners and stitch the hem as for the Tablecloth on page 10.

2 *To cut the stencil:* Locate the stencil designs. Lay the clear plastic sheet over the design and trace it onto the plastic with the fine felt-tipped pen. Place the plastic sheet on the cutting surface and cut out the areas which will be painted, using the craft knife or scalpel. You can make two separate stencils, one for each colour used. To do this, trace the complete design onto both sheets of plastic but cut out each one for a single colour only. The rest of the

traced design will help you position the stencil.

3 *For painting the stencil:* Position the motifs in the corners of your fabric. Note that the napkins are stencilled in one corner only and the border goes around all four sides. Hold the stencil in place with small strips of masking tape. If you are using a single stencil for both colours, it is helpful to cover adjoining areas of the other colour with masking tape. Pour a small quantity of paint into a saucer and spread it out. Stencils require very little paint compared to other painting techniques. Using a dry brush and a dabbing, rather than a stroking, movement paint in the design, working from the edges towards the centre of an area. Wipe off any excess paint. Too much paint on the brush or even a wet brush will cause the paint to seep under the edges of the stencil and give an indistinct outline. Allow the paint to dry between colours to avoid running. Additional highlights can be painted over the top of the stencilled design to give depth and texture to the shapes, for example we painted over yellow with a deeper orange. Keep your stencil clean – wash it between uses, especially if you

are using one stencil for both colours.

4 *To stencil the border:* Work out your colour and pattern distribution before you begin painting. Stencil all around first with one colour, allow it to dry then replace the stencil in the spaces you have left and fill in the second colour. Try moving the stencil for different angles of flowers and leaves, and taking elements out of the design and repositioning them. The stencilled border should link up with the bunch of flowers on both sides.

5 *For the embroidery:* Stitch around the leaves and flowers using Blanket stitch as shown in the Stitch Guide at the front of the book. Choose colours to match the colours of the paints. Remember you want this stitching to be visible so don't make the individual stitches too small. Be sure to follow the edges of the flowers and leaves accurately.

Charming Cross Stitch

Of all the embroidery stitches, Cross stitch is the most popular. Use it on a sampler, a tapestry or a delicately embroidered linen handkerchief and matching jewellery cushion.

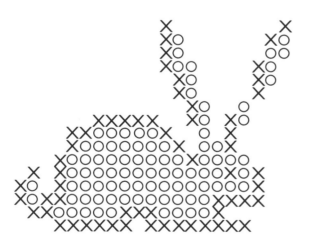

MONOGRAMMED HANDKERCHIEF

The perfect gifts to embroider for someone special, this dainty handkerchief and jewellery cushion are sure to be treasured for a long time. You can make your own handkerchief or buy one to embroider.

MATERIALS

a square of handkerchief linen
wide single edged lace to trim the edge
10 cm square of waste canvas
stranded embroidery thread in the
*   colours of your choice*
a suitable embroidery needle

METHOD

See the Cross stitch alphabet graph on pages 106 and 107.

1 *For the lace:* Draw threads from each edge of the linen square and re-trim to make certain all the edges are perfectly straight. Press in 5 mm all around the square. Stitch the lace under the pressed edge, pleating or gathering it at the corners.

2 *For the embroidery:* Baste the edges of a piece of waste canvas, large enough to accommodate your letter, over one corner of the handkerchief. Locate the letter you require on pages 106 and 107 and embroider it over the waste canvas, through the linen as well, using three strands of embroidery thread. When the embroidery is complete, carefully draw out the canvas, thread by thread, leaving the Cross stitch motif on the linen.

JEWELLERY CUSHION

MATERIALS

two pieces of linen each 13 cm x
*   10 cm*
two strips of linen each 10 cm x 5 cm
two strips of linen each 13 cm x 5 cm
10 cm square of waste canvas
stranded embroidery thread in the
*   colours of your choice*
1.3 m coloured twisted cord
small quantity of polyester fibre for
*   stuffing*
iron on interfacing
matching sewing thread
a suitable embroidery needle

METHOD

See the Cross stitch alphabet graph on pages 106 and 107.
1 cm seams allowed all around each pattern piece.

1 *For the embroidery:* Find the centre of one square of linen by folding it in half lengthways and widthways. The intersection of the folds is the centre point. Baste the edges of a piece of waste canvas, large enough to accommodate your letter, over this centre point. Locate the letter you require on pages 106 and 107 and embroider it over the waste canvas, through the linen as well, using three strands of embroidery thread. When the embroidery is complete, carefully draw out the canvas thread by thread, leaving the Cross stitch motif on the linen.

2 *For the sewing:* Interface all pieces of linen. Pin the short ends of all the strips together to form an open box. Check that it fits around the edge of the embroidered linen. Adjust the

STITCHES USED
Cross stitch for all motifs

Above: Jewellery Cushion
Right: Monogrammed Handkerchief

length if necessary. Pin the strip around the edge of the embroidered linen, with raw edges even, right sides facing and seams matching to the corners. Stitch in a 1 cm seam. Pin the remaining piece of linen to the remaining edge of the strip with right sides together, raw edges even and seams matching to the corners again. Stitch, leaving an opening for turning. Turn the cushion to the right side, pushing the corners out neatly. Stuff the cushion firmly and close the opening by hand. Hand sew the twisted cord around the top edge of the cushion, taking it into three small loops at each corner, resembling a clover leaf. Start and finish at a corner, tucking the ends of the cord out of sight behind a loop at the end.

CORNELLI
WOOL EMBROIDERY

This is a very simple yet effective trim for any woollen garment – and it can be used on lighter fabrics too. Cornelli work is the effect of one long continuous line of stitching, forming a pattern of loops and curves.

STITCHES USED
Chain stitch

MATERIALS

a purchased woollen jumper
suitable yarn for working the stitches
tapestry needle

METHOD

See the cornelli design on page 100.

1 *For the design:* Mark out your pattern area with basting. If you are not confident enough to make the design as you go, mark out your cornelli lines with a soft lead pencil or chalk. You will find it becomes much easier with a little practice. Use the design given here as a guide.

2 *For the embroidery:* The basic stitch used in the embroidery is Chain stitch, though any 'straight' stitch can be effective. We chose Chain stitch as it is fairly bulky and results come quickly. Two different weights of yarn were used – one a textured chenille knitting yarn and another knitting yarn made from smooth glossy silk. Stitch two parallel lines in a random wavy line that keeps turning back on itself until the basted area is covered.

3 *To finish off:* Consider changing the buttons on your cardigan to complement the embroidery. Make the shape of your embroidery suit your garment. For a small area such as a shoulder or the point at centre front, bring the stitching into a point where you can later attach a tassel made from yarn to complete the effect!

Left: See how Cornelli work is simply the effect of two wiggly lines of Chain stitch working together to form the pattern

QUILTING

The charm of an old patchwork quilt can't be explained by the sum of its parts. Whether it is a simple pattern of large squares sewn and tied, or a masterpiece of tiny pieces with beautiful quilting, the quilt has a special appeal because it is a unique piece of work, at once decorative and useful and often made with the heart as well as the hands. In a materialistic world, it also has the appeal of something that money can't buy.

The earliest patchwork quilts were made by frugal, rural women who stitched utilitarian bed covers from saved pieces of worn-out garments, or scraps from other projects. Later, mill workers in Britain, North America and Australia used samples from woollen mills. Sometimes these quilts were roughly sewn, but usually with an eye to the pleasing effect produced by placing one colour or tone against another.

Ladies of greater means saved precious pieces of special fabrics – chintzes, silks and satins, to make beautiful appliqué, pieced and crazy patchwork quilts.

The mosaic type of patchwork is probably the earliest style, developing an all-over effect from simple templates, such as hexagons, which were often pieced over papers. The medallion style, which was built up around the central square, was common in England. Now in the Australian National Gallery, the quilt made by convict women on the ship Rajah, is a good example.

In America, the method of sewing together identical blocks was highly developed into a folk art. The early pieced patterns, such as Log Cabin and Star of Bethlehem, which crossed the Atlantic with early settlers, were adapted and new designs flourished. The revival of interest in quiltmaking, especially since the United States Bicentenary, has been remarkable and reflects a new appreciation of traditional skills.

The making of a quilt needs only simple sewing skills – a running stitch for hand-piecing and hand-quilting, slipstitch for binding and a straight machine stitch for piecing blocks and sewing on bindings. It is a help to have a good eye for straight lines, or at least some respect for the grain of the fabric.

The art in quiltmaking lies in choosing a design and fabrics that are complementary and pleasing. Spend the time to consider these elements before starting. There is something very satisfying in completing a quilt, not the least of which is that it will last. A simple design of squares, machine-pieced and tied is quick to make and will add visual delight to a room. A simply pieced design, with lots of fine hand-quilting may take a long time to make, but it will have an heirloom quality that a mass-produced bedcover can never imitate. An added bonus to the quilter is the time it allows to contemplate while quilting – a wonderful luxury in a busy world.

Margot Child

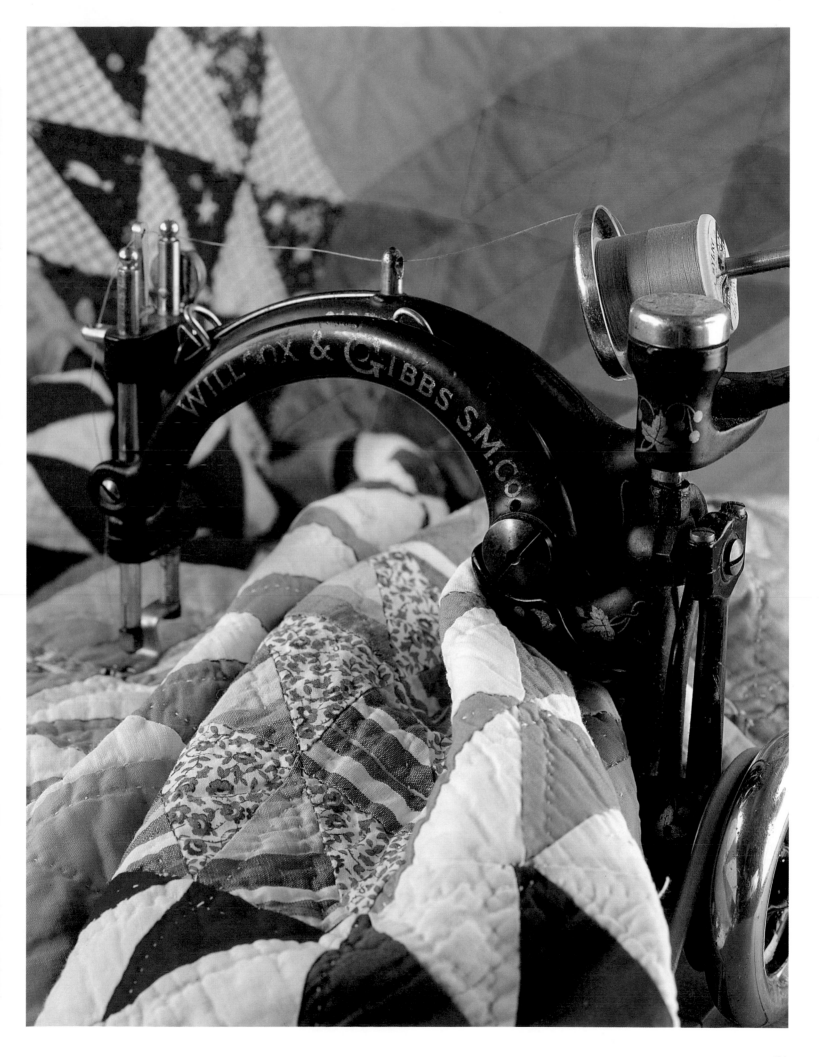

The Quilt
Story

Quilting is both an art, rich in
creativity, and a craft with all the
pleasures of working on a project
with skill and quiet enjoyment.

The Quilter's Cupboard

Just like any other craft, successful quilting depends on having the right equipment to do the job. If you are already a sewer, you are more than likely to have some of the things you need at home already – such as a tape measure, needles, scissors and so on. There are, however, a few pieces you will need to buy and it's a good idea to buy the best that you can afford when it comes to equipment you will want to use again and again. There is nothing more frustrating than trying to cut along a straight line with a pair of blunt scissors. You'll chew up so much fabric that it would have been cheaper to buy good scissors in the beginning.

This is a list of the equipment you are likely to need, although you may not need everything on the list for every quilt.

SCISSORS

A good pair of scissors is essential and ideally you should have three pairs, including a large pair of dressmaker's shears, a smaller pair for delicate cutting and the fiddly bits, and a third pair for cutting paper and templates. It is a good idea to reserve your good dressmaker's shears for cutting fabric, to keep them in the best condition.

PINS

Glass-headed pins are ideal for patchwork and quilting. You may like to use pins of different lengths for different purposes. Longer pins are handy for pinning through a number of layers of fabric and batting. Even better than ordinary pins for this purpose, are medium-sized safety pins which hold the work together quite securely and are a speedier solution than basting with a needle and thread. We call this pin-basting.

NEEDLES

For hand-piecing, use a fine needle you are comfortable with. Sharps are suitable for the purpose. For hand-quilting, you will need size 8 or 9 Betweens. As these are quite short there will be times when you may need a longer needle as well and Sharps are again suitable.

For machine-piecing and machine-quilting, you will need a machine needle suitable for the thickness of your fabrics. Be ruthless – throw away needles as soon as they lose their sharpness. In fact, it is a good idea to begin each project with a new needle.

CUTTER

The rotary or Olfa cutter is a great boon to the quilter. A great labour saver, it allows you to cut several layers of fabric at one time without distortion. You should use a rotary cutter in conjunction with a good plastic ruler and a self-healing mat, made especially for the purpose.

RULERS

Avoid wooden rulers and choose one made from plastic or metal instead. The plastic ones have the dual advantages of being quite sturdy and allowing you to see through the ruler to the fabric or paper beneath.

Craft shops sell excellent plastic rulers especially made for quilting that have several marked reference points to assist you to cut straight and accurately. The drawback with these rulers is that they are marked in imperial measurements, so you will need to convert all your measurements. There is a comprehensive Metric/Imperial Conversion chart on page 15.

SEWING MACHINE

Consider your sewing machine as an extension of yourself while stitching a quilt! Your machine needs to be clean and oiled at all times to keep it running properly, and your machine needle needs replacing frequently. Bernina machines with a knee-lift lever for the presser foot are a positive gift to quilters, as they allow you to keep two hands on your work at all times.

THIMBLES

Smooth quilting technique always demands that you use at least one thimble and perhaps two – a metal one for the third finger of the upper hand and a leather one for the finger underneath to protect it.

THREAD

Good quality machine thread should be used for hand or machine-piecing. For hand-quilting, it is best to use cotton quilting thread. It is stronger than the usual machine thread and comes in a good variety of colours. In the past, threads have been treated by passing them through beeswax (some books still recommend it) but it is no longer necessary with the excellent quilting threads available today.

The colour of the thread for piecing should blend with the fabrics so you can work with only one colour and not have to keep re-threading the needle. You can buy nylon monofilament thread at good quilting shops. This has the advantage of being 'invisible' and therefore suitable for all colours. It should be used as the top thread only, with an ordinary machine sewing thread in the bobbin.

PENCILS

A soft, sharp lead pencil for tracing around templates is essential. These days you can buy water-soluble pencils and pens, especially made for quilters, including a silver pencil that will mark both light and dark fabrics. Make sure that whatever you choose will either fade out or wash out without leaving a permanent mark.

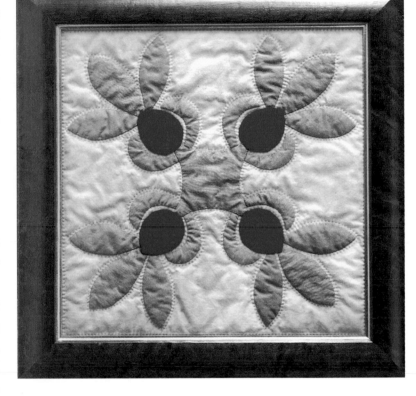
Supplied by Natalie Wise

TEMPLATES

A template is a precisely drawn and cut shape for a pattern piece. Some templates for hand-piecing, such as the shell, hexagon and diamond, are available from craft shops but it is not difficult to make your own. If the template is not going to be used too often, then cardboard (perhaps strengthened with tape) is quite suitable. Sandpaper is also useful as it tends to grip the fabric as you work. The problem with both of these options is that they are very subject to wear and tear, especially around the edges. If you do use cardboard, it is a good idea to cut a number of templates rather than relying on just one. If the template is going to be used many times or if the particular project is a big one, then you would be wise to cut your template out of firm plastic or acetate, available from quilting and art supply shops. Whichever material you choose, you will need the usual drawing aids (set square, protractor, pencil, ruler etc) as well as a sharp craft knife or scissors for cutting out the template. Draw your shape carefully onto the template material, using a ruler to achieve straight lines. Carefully cut out the shape with a sharp craft knife or scissors. In this book, templates for tracing are supplied.

HOOPS AND FRAMES

Quilting hoops are essential on all but the smallest hand-quilted projects to achieve a smooth finish. A quilting hoop consists of two wooden rings, one of which fits closely inside the other. The fabric is stretched over the inner ring and then secured with the outer ring. Take care not to stretch the fabric too tightly. A hoop of about 40 cm is a good size to work with. You can also buy a quilting hoop on a stand or, if the project is a large one, use a free-standing quilting frame if you find one comfortable to work with. You can also buy small hoops, specially made for machine-quilting.

MATERIAL MATTERS

You can always tell a true quilter by the bulging bags and drawers full of fascinating scraps of fabric, squirrelled away for future use. And actually, this is one of the most delightful aspects of quilting – that even when you're not actually working on a project, you can be planning and designing, waiting for the coincidence of two scraps of fabric to trigger your imagination.

CHOOSING YOUR FABRIC

A quilt is basically a sandwich with a filling, the batting or wadding, between two layers of fabric. The filling is held in place by the stitches of the quilting or by the tying. Any fabric which keeps its shape when stretched with two hands along the grain can be used for quilting.

The choice of fabrics and colours is crucial to the success of a quilt. You can use patterns and plains of just about every kind, but some fabrics are obviously better suited than others. Smooth, closely woven, dress-weight cottons are ideal for quilting. Linen, lightweight wool, silk or sateen also work well. Avoid synthetic or stretchy fabrics as they are more difficult to manage. Velvet gives a lovely texture to patchwork, but you will need a little more experience to manage its foibles. Whichever you choose, make sure all your fabrics are of the same, or very similar, weight.

Some quite heavy fabrics, like tweed or wool, can look very effective, but are a great challenge for the hand-quilter. It is best to reserve these for machine-quilting. At the other end of the scale, very sheer fabrics can also give you quilters' nightmares! If you must use one because it is just right and there is no substitute, line it first with a dress-weight cotton.

Small prints, florals and checks are ideal for quilting, but bolder prints can also be effective. To get an impression of how the finished quilt will look, drape the fabrics over a chair in roughly the proportions you will be using them and then stand back and consider. You will be able to tell how well the colours and patterns work together or whether you need to make changes. Stripes can be very effective, but take care – they will show any faults if your cutting and sewing are not perfectly straight. The difference between a mediocre quilt and an outstanding one is often because of the way

the quilter has used light, shade and colour to complement the patchwork. Experiment with combinations of colour and pattern – you will learn with experience which combinations work best.

BACKING

Choose a pure cotton fabric for the quilt back, washing and preparing it in the same way as the fabrics for the quilt top. For a large quilt, you may have to join fabrics to achieve the width of backing required. If you are new to quilting, choose a print fabric for the backing rather than a plain one – it is much more forgiving of the odd uneven stitch.

PREPARING YOUR FABRIC

It is crucial to wash (preferably in a washing machine) cotton fabrics before you cut. Washing will pre-shrink the fabric and take out the excess dye and any chemical sizing. The dye in some fabrics can run and stain the others, so wash any likely culprits by hand to test for colour fastness. Iron the fabrics while they are still damp. Remove all the selvages before you begin cutting.

BATTING

Batting, or wadding as it is also known, is the filling in the 'quilt sandwich'. In days past, any thick material, such as flannel or even an old quilt, was used for batting. These days the most commonly used batting is made from polyester fibre. It is available in a variety of widths and thicknesses and has the advantage of being lightweight, washable and non-allergenic. Traditional cotton batting is still used but is much heavier than the polyester version and the finished quilt will have to be dry cleaned. Take care with cotton batting because it tends to move around and bunch up in spots. Close quilting will help to prevent this happening. Batting which is not too hard to the touch is the easiest to sew. It should be bonded to prevent fibres migrating through the quilt.

Wool batting gives a wonderful warmth and softness to a quilt. Cotton/polyester batting is also available. Like your quilting fabrics, it has to be pre-washed as the cotton content shrinks. For hand-quilting, it is better to choose the thinner batting, which gives the traditional look, and keep the thicker types for machine-quilted and tied quilts, which sometimes look more like comforters.

QUILTING SKILLS

Quilting is not difficult. If you can sew a simple running stitch, you can make a quilt. There are a few simple principles and techniques which will help you.

MARKING FABRIC

Always mark the fabric on the wrong side with a sharp pencil, dark for light fabric and light or silver for dark fabric. Test the marker for washability on a scrap of fabric first. Place the template on the fabric with a straight edge following the grainline. Some templates will even have the grainline marked for you.

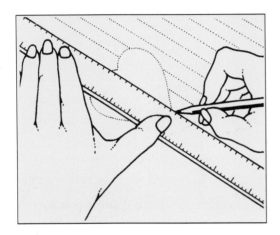

Left: Use a plastic ruler and sharp pencil to mark lines and templates on your fabric

CUTTING OUT

Pieced quilting requires the cutting of dozens of small shapes. The quickest way to cut a quantity of the same piece is to cut three or four thicknesses of fabric together. Using a rotary cutter and cutting mat is the easiest way to cut strips. Otherwise you will need to

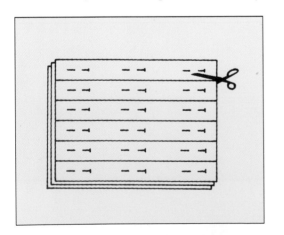

Left: Cutting out a large number of strips using the multi-layered method

pin the fabric layers together, placing the pins inside the cutting line which is marked on the top layer. Cut out the shape carefully with good, sharp scissors,

taking particular care with the corners. This method is suitable only if you can work without marked seamlines. For all hand-piecing and some machine-piecing, pencilled seamlines are essential. Trace around the template with a sharp pencil then cut out with a seam allowance added, usually 6 mm. The pencil lines you have drawn become your sewing line.

SEWING

There are two easy quilting principles you should follow:

1 Sew in straight lines and avoid sewing into corners if possible.

2 Join small pieces together to form larger ones and then join those into even larger ones and continue in this way. Often you will sew several steps to make the basic block of the quilt and then join the blocks together to complete the quilt top.

Pieces are always joined with right sides facing, except for appliqué.

MACHINE-PIECING OR HAND-PIECING

Machine-piecing is the quickest way of joining patchwork but there are occasions when handsewing is preferable, such as when you need to sew in angles or carefully match difficult points. Equally, some quilts are best machine-pieced, such as the *Log Cabin* and *Seminole* designs. In truth, quilters who choose hand-piecing do so, not for practical reasons, but for the pleasure of relaxing hand work and its portability.

Before you begin sewing, you will need to establish a reference for the seam allowance. If the distance from the needle to the edge of the presser

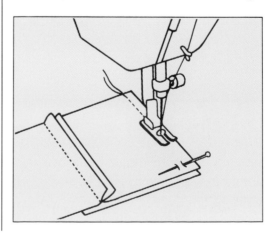

Left: Machine-piecing patches together into a strip

foot is 6 mm, then you can place the edge of the presser foot on the edge of the fabric to achieve the exact seam allowance. If this is not the case on your machine, you can use any lines marked on the foot plate or mark your own with masking tape.

Pin the pieces together with right sides facing, placing the pins at right angles to the seamline. There is no need to backstitch at this stage because seams will be crossed over by others. Sew the patches together along the seamline, sewing right up to the

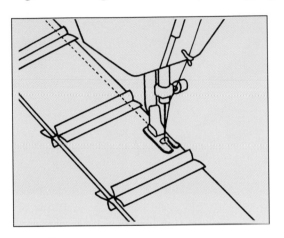

Left: Piecing strips together, sewing across the seams

pins. When you have joined patches into a square or strip, you will need to join that square or strip to others and this will involve sewing across seamlines. Pin and sew as before, taking care to match seamlines and points.

To save time, sew all the same steps for the whole quilt at once, feeding them under the presser foot in a continuous seam. Later, you can cut them apart before joining them in a new combination by the

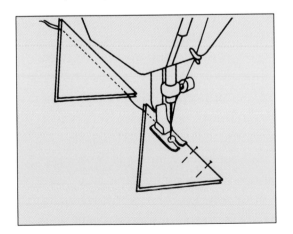

Left: Chainsewing triangles to form pieced squares

same method – chainsewing.

Hand-piecing is the traditional method of joining patchwork both with and without papers. The quilts in this book are all made without papers. Pin the patches together with right sides facing, placing the pins at right angles to the seamline. Sew with small

even running stitches, using a size 8 or 9 Sharp needle and quilting cotton (or cotton-covered polyester) thread. Take care not to have your thread too long – about 40 cm is enough. Begin and end the seam with a few backstitches to secure it. When joining patches, take care to match the pencil lines (seamlines) on both sides, sew only between seamlines and do not stitch in the seam allowances.

PRESSING

Always press seams as you work to keep the pieces flat and the seams as sharp as possible. If you are working with very thick fabric, press the seams open. Generally, however, seams pressed to one side are stronger than those pressed open. Press the seam allowances towards the darker fabric to prevent them showing through the lighter one. Take care not to stretch pieces out of shape when pressing.

CONSTRUCTION

Cut the batting and backing a little larger than the finished size required as the quilting itself draws the fabrics in. You can join lengths of backing fabric to achieve the width you require, after removing all the selvages. Press the seam allowances to one side. The backing can be the same size as the quilt top and then all the edges bound together with a separate binding, or you can have the backing fabric fold onto the quilt front to make a self-binding.

To assemble your quilt, lay the backing fabric face down on a table. Place the batting over the top and then the quilt top on top of that, face up. Smooth out any wrinkles and pin the layers together using medium-sized safety pins or baste for hand-quilting if you prefer.

If you are basting, begin at the centre of the quilt and sew towards each corner. Then sew in rows about 10 cm apart over the whole quilt.

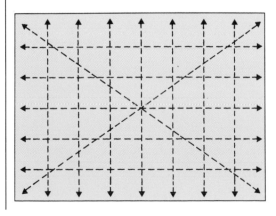

Left: The basting pattern for securing the layers of the quilt

BORDERS

Not all quilts have borders. Some patterns are traditionally made without one, but a border can be used to embellish as well as enlarge a quilt. You can have more than one border. Before you attach the borders, press the quilt top well. Remember that the border should look like an integral part of the design, not an afterthought. Choose a fabric that complements the others in the quilt. To work out the length of your side border strips, measure the quilt top lengthways through the centre – not along the edges. Cut two borders of the desired width to this length. After attaching the side borders, measure the total width of the quilt top, including the side borders, and cut the top and bottom borders to this length. If you wish to mitre the border corners, cut the strips extra long, centre them on each edge of the quilt, sew them on, then join them with a seam at an angle of 45-degrees at each corner.

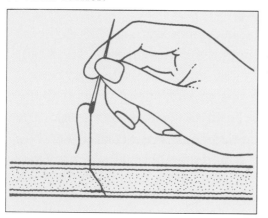

Left: Secure the knotted end of your thread by pulling it into the batting

QUILTING

Quilting by hand should be done using a quilting hoop to keep the layers secure while you work. Use quilting thread colour-matched to the fabric unless you want the stitching to show for a special effect. Thread a size 7 or 8 Between sewing needle with about 40 cm of thread and tie a knot in the end. Begin stitching in the centre of the quilt, inserting the

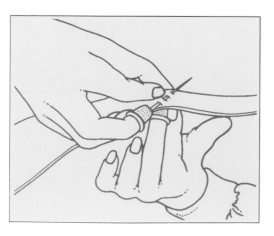

Left: Hand-quilting requires two thimbles for a smooth technique

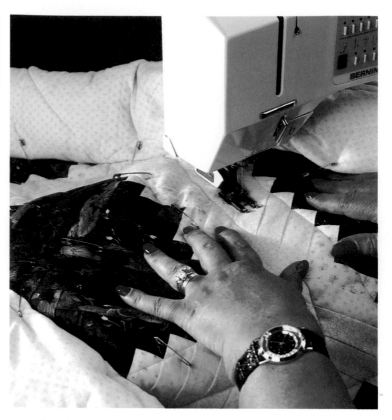

needle about 2 cm from where you wish to begin. Pull gently on the thread so the knot slips into the batting. Work in small, even running stitches, sewing around the seamlines, outline quilting 6 mm inside the edges of the patches or in patterns that you have drawn onto the fabric. Use a stencil to keep your patterns uniform over the whole of the quilt. When you have finished quilting, end as you began by knotting the thread and running it about 2 cm into the batting before cutting it off, even with the fabric. To move from one motif to another, take the needle under the top layer of your quilt rather than cutting the thread and beginning again.

Machine-quilting is becoming more and more popular. While results appear very quickly, it does have the disadvantage of not being portable. Use a cotton-coated polyester machine sewing thread or a nylon monofilament thread and a size 70 to 90 needle, depending on the thickness of your quilt. You may also need to adjust the stitch length. Do a little test piece to check all your settings. An even-feed walking foot attachment will help to move the layers of your quilt smoothly without effort or bunching. As with hand-quilting, you should begin in the centre of your quilt and work towards the edges. To do this, roll the opposite sides up quite tightly on either side of the presser foot leaving the area to be quilted lying flat in the middle. You can then unroll parts as you need them.

BINDING

When all the quilting is complete, trim back the batting and backing to be even with the quilt top (unless you are going to fold the backing over onto the front to make self binding). Cut your binding

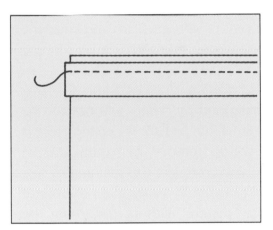

Left: Applying the binding to the top edge of the quilt

strips to the width suggested and the length required for the top, bottom and sides of the quilt, measured through the centre. Fold the strips over double with wrong sides together. Press. Stitch the binding to the sides of the quilt, through all thicknesses, with

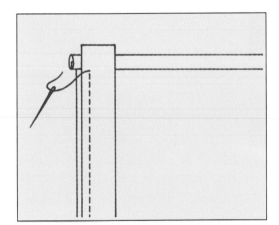

Left: Applying the binding to the side of the quilt, over the top of the previously joined top binding

right sides together and raw edges even. Fold the binding over to the back of the quilt and handsew it into position. Repeat for the top and bottom edges.

MITRING A CORNER

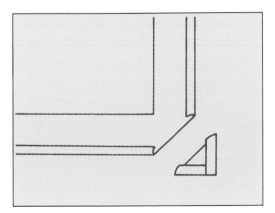

Left: Fold in the raw edge and cut off the corner

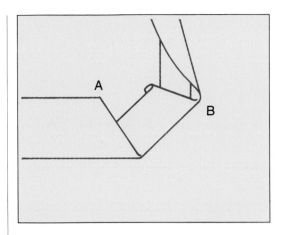

Left: fold in the corner

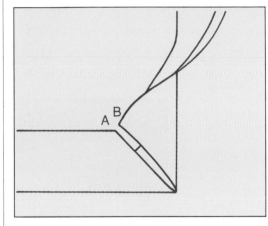

Left: Fold in half the side edges, then fold in the other half so that A meets B

TUFTING OR TYING QUILTS

Some large quilts are not quilted at all in the traditional sense, but are tied. This is particularly useful for quilts where a very thick batting has been used. Using heavy crochet cotton, take a stitch through all the

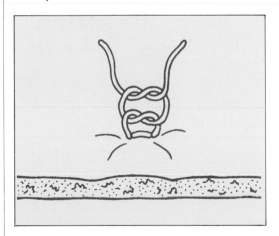

Left: Using thick cotton to tie a quilt

layers of the quilt. Tie the ends together securely twice, but don't pull too tightly. Trim the ends. For very dramatic tufts, use several strands of thread or very thick thread. You can tie a quilt using matching or contrasting cotton. Tie in the seamline or in the centre of the patch, depending on whether you are making a feature of the tying or not. You can tie your quilt on the top, or on the back if you do not wish the tufts to show.

Applique Quilts

Appliqué adds a new dimension to traditional quilting. It can add texture and pattern to a simple single-piece quilt or embellish a pieced quilt, making it a truly unique object.

Appliqué has been known for centuries and for much of that time it has been part of the quilter's art. The advent of inexpensive printed cotton fabrics gave an almost limitless range to the possibilities. One area in which this development was most obvious was in the flourishing of Broderie Perse quilts. This is a technique in which suitable motifs are cut from printed chintz fabric and appliquéd onto a background fabric which can itself be pieced and decorated with stencils and appliqué.

The delight of appliqué is that you can use any pattern or design that takes your fancy. There are many traditional designs that are often seen in appliqué quilts, but be adventurous – design your own. A motif from wallpaper, a picture from a book, a design in a shop window are all useful sources. The photocopier and enlarger at work or at your local library will be your greatest ally when it comes to designing your appliqué quilt.

HAND-APPLIQUE

There are a number of methods of hand-appliqué, the most common ones involving the use of paper patterns. It is important if you are using a repeating appliqué that the shape and size of the piece does not vary too much – that is, of course, unless you want it to. To ensure this uniformity, the quilter makes a paper pattern of the appliqué shape, traces the shape onto the wrong side of the fabric (tracing many of them at a time and adding seam allowances if they are not already included) and cuts them out. If you do not have access to a light box to do your tracing, taping the fabric to a sunlit window will usually do quite well. Pin a paper pattern, following grainlines, to the back of each traced pattern and cut out

with a 6 mm seam allowance. Baste the pattern to the fabric, removing the pins as you go. Turn and baste the seam allowance to the wrong side with a small running stitch. Press.

When placing your appliqué pieces, remember that those which are overlapped by others will need to be attached first using a small whipstitch. When the piece is amost completely sewn on, remove the basting and the paper pattern before you complete the stitching. A pair of tweezers is ideal for carefully pulling out the paper pattern without disturbing the stitching. When all the appliqué pieces have been attached, press the quilt top carefully.

If your appliqué piece is quite large and bulky or if the background fabric is showing through, you can cut out the background from the back, leaving a 6 mm border all around.

Doffy White, who made this wonderful appliqué quilt, made her templates out of pliable plastic so they could easily be removed and re-used without her having to cut hundreds of small paper pieces. She repeated the charming appliqué design in the hand-quilting.

MACHINE-APPLIQUE

Appliqué with a sewing machine is quick and easy. It is crucial to know your sewing machine and all its foibles and to keep it in top working order. Always use sharp needles and keep the machine well oiled. If you have a special walking foot that feeds the fabric evenly through the machine you will find your work even easier. You can also buy a quilting guide for accurate stitching.

You can machine-appliqué using a paper pattern as for hand-appliqué or you can use the Broderie Perse method. In either case, a small zigzag stitch is ideal for stitching the motifs to your quilt. Iron-on interfacing or bonding web is used by some quilters to attach their motifs before stitching. Experiment to find the method that best suits you and your quilt.

METRIC/IMPERIAL CONVERSION CHART

All the measurements in this book are given in metric. If you prefer to work in imperial measurements, or if your equipment is marked in imperial measurements, use this chart to convert from one to the other. The conversions can only be the closest approximation, so it is crucial that you work only in imperial OR metric – not both. It does not matter which one you choose as long as you stay with your choice all the way through.

6 mm	$^1/_4$ in	25 cm	10 in
1 cm	$^1/_2$ in	30 cm	12 in
12 mm	$^1/_2$ in	35 cm	14 in
1.5 cm	$^3/_4$ in	40 cm	16 in
2 cm	$^3/_4$ in	45 cm	18 in
3 cm	$1^1/_4$ in	50 cm	20 in
4 cm	$1^1/_2$ in	60 cm	24 in
5 cm	2 in	70 cm	28 in
6 cm	$2^1/_2$ in	80 cm	32 in
7 cm	3 in	90 cm	36 in
8 cm	$3^1/_4$ in	1 m	40 in
9 cm	$3^1/_2$ in	115 cm	45 in
10 cm	4 in	150 cm	60 in
12 cm	$4^3/_4$ in	2 m	$2^1/_4$ yds
13 cm	$5^1/_4$ in	2.5 m	$2^3/_4$ yds
15 cm	6 in	3 m	$3^1/_4$ yds
17 cm	7 in	4 m	$4^1/_2$ yds
20 cm	8 in	5 m	$5^1/_2$ yds

Traditional Quilts

For *centuries, piecing fabrics together into quilts of intricate design has been a much-loved craft. Few examples of the earliest patchwork quilts remain, but the more recent history is richly illustrated with beautiful pieces such as these.*

LOG CABIN QUILTS

Log Cabin quilts are among the most popular traditional quilt patterns. Follow Kate McEwen's step-by-step guide to making your own Log Cabin quilt on the following pages.

Log Cabin quilts are ideal for beginners and the pattern can be easily adapted to smaller projects such as cushions, pot holders and placemats. Our step-by-step quilt is a *Log Cabin* quilt in the *Barn Raising* style, one of the most popular quilt patterns. It can be a true scrapbag quilt, utilising quite small pieces of fabric where the only governing factor is the contrast between light and dark colours.

Like all *Log Cabin* quilts, it is based on the pattern of light and dark rectangles, pieced around a centre square. The rectangles are laid in such a way as to represent the logs used by the early American settlers to build their cabins. Some early quilts even had a little chimney sewn in to further underline the theme. The centre square of the block is often red, to denote the fireplace, or yellow, to represent the lighted window.

These days, most *Log Cabin* quilts are made from light and dark printed, dress-weight cottons but, in the past, quilters often used wool as well. Mixing silks, velvets, and other 'luxury' fabrics produces a lovely quilt with quite a different feeling about it. Traditional *Log Cabin* quilts were made without a border, but this is not a hard-and-fast rule and these days quilters often add a plain or print border.

While the basic ingredients of a *Log Cabin* block remain the same – half in light and half in dark rectangles, changing the way in which the rectangles are placed or the blocks are joined will give you quite a different looking quilt. Joining the blocks so that the dark halves are adjacent to one another and the light halves are adjacent to one another, gives a design of alternating light and dark diamonds. Piecing the blocks and joining them so that the dark and light halves form alternating diagonals, reminiscent of a roof line, makes this design known as *Barn Raising*. Placing the blocks so that the dark and light halves travel diagonally across the quilt creates the pattern known as *Straight Furrow*. Making a block so that the light and dark quarters are opposite their mates, and joining the blocks side by side across the row, makes yet another pattern called *Courthouse Steps*.

Left: Make this Log Cabin quilt following the instructions on pages 20-23

Left: A charming Log Cabin quilt combining subtle colours and prints for a real country look

Below left: This charming placemat is simply one Log Cabin block with a stencilled design painted into the centre square. To complete the placemat, assemble the top, batting, backing and binding as for a quilt

Below: Log Cabin quilts depend on the arrangement of light and dark fabrics for their effect

CREATE A QUILT

FINISHED SIZE

Quilt: 180 cm x 225 cm
(approximately)
Block size: 22.5 cm (approximately)
Total number of full blocks: 48

FABRIC QUANTITIES

20 cm of colour 1 (red)
20 cm of colour 2 (dark)
30 cm of colour 3 (light)
40 cm of colour 4 (dark)
45 cm of colour 5 (light)
55 cm of colour 6 (dark)
1.5 m of colour 7 (light), this includes
     fabric for the first border
1.2 m of colour 8 (dark), this includes
     fabric for the second border
185 cm x 230 cm backing fabric,
     pieced from 4.6 m of 115 cm
     wide fabric
185 cm x 230 cm wadding
     an additional 60 cm of colour 8
     for the binding

NOTIONS

safety pins, pins, needles and scissors
sewing thread
sewing machine
pencil and ruler
rotary (Olfa) cutter and mat

CUTTING

6 mm seam allowances are included in
the cutting instructions.

1 You will need to cut your fabric
into strips by folding the fabric in
half, selvage to selvage, and then
again so you have four layers. If you
are using a rotary (Olfa) cutter you can
put about three lots of fabric, folded
this way, on top of each other and cut
them all at once. An Olfa cutter is
ideal for a *Log Cabin* quilt and means
that seam allowances are already
included in the cutting instructions.
Cut all the fabric into 4 cm strips. You
will need:
2 strips of red, cut into 4 cm squares
5 strips of colour 2
7 strips of colour 3
9 strips of colour 4
11 strips of colour 5
13 strips of colour 6
16 strips of colour 7
19 strips of colour 8

Step 2

CONSTRUCTION

2 Take the pile of red squares and
one strip of colour 2. Lay the strip
under the presser foot of your sewing

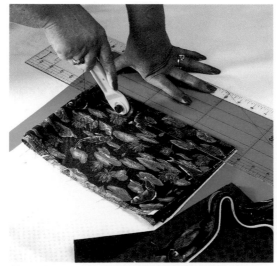

Step 1: Using a specially
marked plastic ruler, rotary
cutter and mat to cut multiple
fabric layers
Step 2: Chainsewing all the
red squares to the first dark
strip

Step 1

machine (right side up) and lay the red squares on top one by one (right side down), stitching them together in a 6 mm seam. Sew all the red squares in this way. Finger press the seams to lie flat and cut the strips apart so you have a red square joined to a colour 2 square.

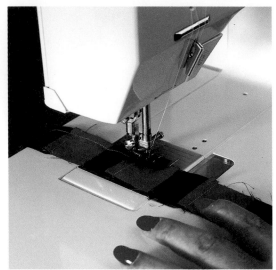

Step 3

3 Take the other strips of colour 2 and lay them down one by one (face up) under your presser foot and sew the previously joined red and colour 2 squares down onto these strips. Always place the segment just sewn at the top when placing the block on the next strip to be sewn. Finger press the seams to lie flat. Cut the newly formed squares apart, even with the edges of the dark and red squares.

Step 4

4 Place the first light strip (colour 3) under the presser foot as you did for the colour 2 strip and join the just completed squares as before. Cut them apart, even with the edges as before. Finger press the seams to lie flat.

5 Add the second strip of colour 3 as before and continue in this way, sewing two strips of the same colour to each square until all the colours have been sewn to the block. Always place at the top the segment just sewn when placing the block on the next strip to be sewn. Finger press the seams to lie flat. Cut the newly formed squares apart, even with the edges of the black and red squares.

Step 5

6 When the forty-eight blocks are complete, arrange them, six blocks across and eight blocks down, as shown for the *Barn Raising* pattern. Sew the blocks together, making sure to match the seams where necessary. Press the quilt top carefully.

7 Attach a border to your quilt if you feel it needs one. Borders can be used to extend a quilt to whatever size you need. We have used two borders – one out of light fabric 8.8 cm wide and the other out of dark fabric 13.8 cm wide. To make the light border, measure the length of your

Step 3: Joining the piece made in Step 2 to another dark strip
Step 4: Using exactly the same procedure as in Step 3, join in the first light strip
Step 5: The completed block for the quilt, with the red square slightly off centre. Note that there are two more dark strips than there are light strips in the block

70

quilt top through the centre. Cut two strips of fabric this length and 10 cm wide. Join fabric if necessary to make the required length. Sew these to the side edges of the quilt top in 6 mm seams. Measure the total width of the quilt top, including the borders you have just joined on, again measuring through the centre. Cut two strips of fabric this length, joining strips if necessary, and 10 cm wide. Sew these to the top and bottom edges of the quilt in 6 mm seams. Make the dark border in exactly the same way, cutting the strips 15 cm wide.

QUILTING

8 Place backing fabric on a table, right side down and sticky tape it down to stop it from slipping. Place the batting on top and then the pieced quilt on top of that, facing upwards. Pin through all three layers with safety pins to hold the quilt together while you are machine or hand-quilting. *Log Cabin* quilts can also be tied in the traditional way. We have quilted this quilt by machine, stitching diagonally through the centre of each block, changing the direction of the diagonal for each quarter of the quilt. Take the stitching through the light border as well. Make another row of stitches in between each pair of rows just made.

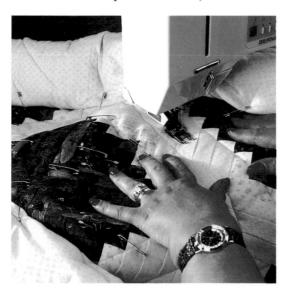

Step 8

The dark border has been quilted with rows of parallel stitching about 5 cm apart. Trim away any excess batting and backing.

FINISHING

9 To bind the edges of the quilt, cut four 8 cm wide strips for the top, bottom and sides. Measure through the centre of the quilt as before to determine the length of the strips. Join strips if necessary to achieve the required length. Press the strips over double with wrong sides together. Sew the binding to the right side of both sides of the quilt with raw edges even. Fold the binding over to the wrong side of the quilt and handsew into place. Repeat the measuring and sewing steps described in Step 7 for the top and bottom binding.

Above: Detail of the diagonal machine-quilting
Step 8: Quilting by machine, showing the quilted parts rolled up out of the way

71

SINGLE IRISH CHAIN

Margot Child designed and made this beautiful quilt which is simplicity itself. Made from only two fabrics, a creamy white and contrasting crisp blue cotton, it relies for its charm on the delicate stitching of the hand-quilting.

FABRIC SUGGESTIONS

The blocks in this quilt are set at an angle, travelling diagonally across the quilt. For a slightly different look, make this quilt in two tones of the same colour.

The quilt has been machine-pieced and hand-quilted.

FINISHED SIZE

Quilt: 215 cm x 190 cm (approximately)
Block size: 15 cm x 15 cm
Total number of blocks: 162
Total number of border triangles: 34
Total number of half triangles: 4

FABRIC QUANTITIES

4 m of 115 cm wide white fabric
2 m of 115 cm wide blue fabric
200 cm x 225 cm backing fabric, pieced from 4 m of 115 cm wide fabric
222 cm x 200 cm batting

NOTIONS

cardboard or template plastic
pencil and ruler
rotary (Olfa) cutter and mat
safety pins, pins, needles and scissors
sewing thread and quilting thread
sewing machine

CUTTING

Do not forget to add seam allowances to each piece you cut.

1 Cut ninety white fabric squares 15 cm x 15 cm plus seam allowances. Cut thirty-eight blue fabric triangles from template **a**, adding seam allowances on all sides. Cut four blue fabric half-triangles from template **b** for the corners adding seam allowances on all sides. Cut strips of blue and white fabric 5 cm wide plus seam allowances.

With this quilt it is particularly important to match the grainlines on the template and fabric in order not to be left with a bias edge on your quilt.

CONSTRUCTION

See the Pull Out Pattern Sheet at the back of the book for the additional quilting designs.

2 Piece the strips together in threes, one-third with two whites and a blue in the middle and two-thirds with two blues and a white in the middle. Press the seams to the blue side. Cut the joined strips into 5 cm lengths plus seam allowances.

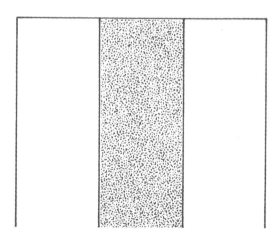

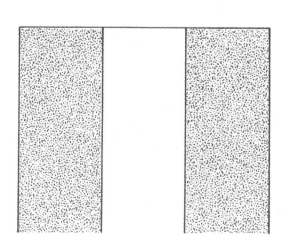

3 Join the strips made in Step 2 in a chequerboard pattern to make seventy-two 9-patch blocks, each with a blue square in the centre. Press.

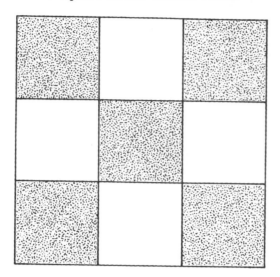

4 Join these blocks to form rows, alternating large white squares with the chequerboard blocks and placing a white square on each end. Press. Note that the number of blocks in a row depends on the position of the row in the quilt. You will need: two single white blocks; two rows of three blocks; two rows of five blocks; two rows of seven blocks; two rows of nine blocks; two rows of eleven blocks; two rows of thirteen blocks; two rows of fifteen blocks and two rows of seventeen blocks.

5 At this point it is a good idea to lay your quilt out as it will look when finished. Pin the short side of a blue triangle to the end of each row, so that the long sides of all the triangles form the straight sides of the quilt. Sew the triangles in place. Press.

6 Join all the rows to form the quilt top, sewing a blue half-triangle to every corner square. Press the quilt top carefully.

QUILTING

7 One quilting design appears on the opposite page, two others are on the pattern sheet. Trace the quilting designs and make stencils/templates of them, using firm plastic. Transfer the designs to the quilt top using the template and a lead pencil.

8 Lay the backing fabric face down on a table. Place the batting on top and then the quilt top, face up, on top of that. Baste or pin-baste all the layers together.

9 Hand-quilt the quilt top, stitching along the pencil lines and approximately 6 mm inside the small squares as shown.

FINISHING

10 Trim the quilt top and batting so that approximately 3 cm of the backing fabric protrudes all around. Turn the backing over onto the quilt top, folding in the corners twice to form a neat mitre (see page 13). Turn under 1 cm on the raw edge and handsew the folded edges and the corners into place.

Left: Detail of the Single Irish Chain quilt showing the hand-quilting

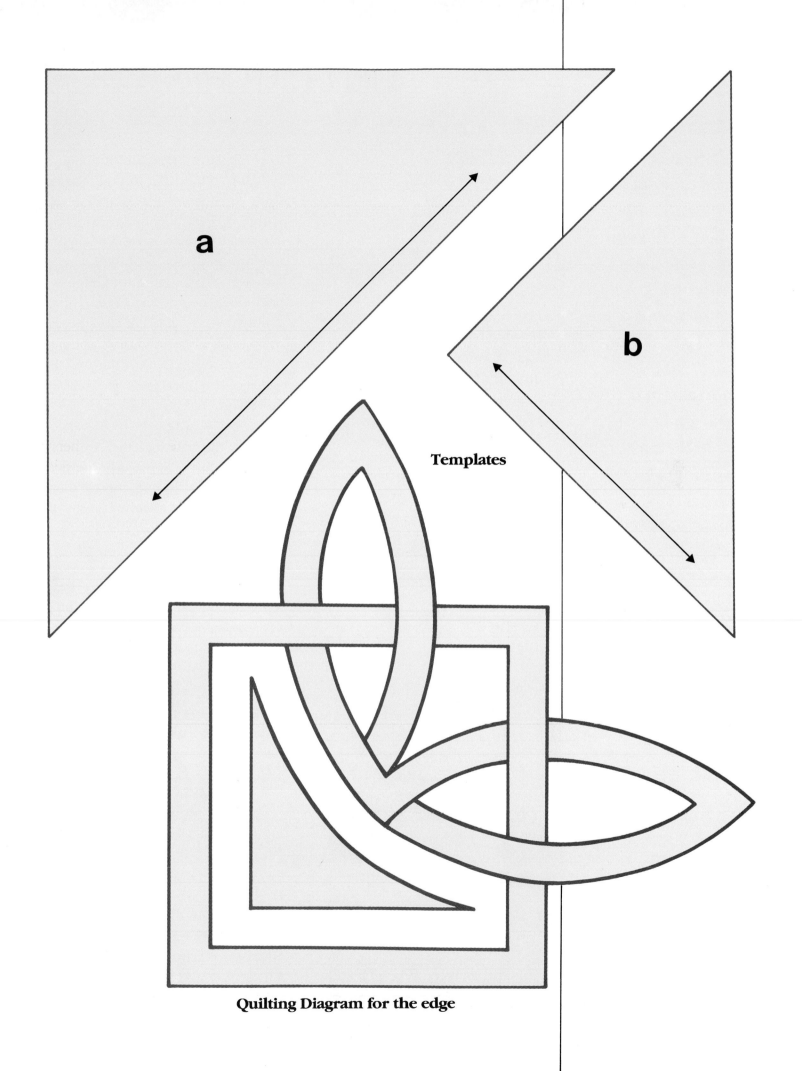

a

b

Templates

Quilting Diagram for the edge

TIED PATCHES

Marie Grove designed and made this quilt by piecing rectangles of brightly coloured cotton and then hand-tying them in the traditional way. You can make this bright and cheerful quilt in a weekend. Quilt it by sewing in the ditches of the seams between the patches or hand-quilting a design over the whole quilt top.

FINISHED SIZE
Quilt: 140 cm x 200 cm
    (approximately)
Block size: 30 cm x 20 cm

FABRIC QUANTITIES
36 rectangles of cotton fabric, in as many colours as possible
150 cm x 210 cm (approximately) backing fabric, pieced from 3 m of 115 cm wide fabric
1.5 m black fabric for the borders and binding
150 cm x 210 cm (approximately) batting

NOTIONS
thick crochet cotton for tying
safety pins, pins, needles and scissors
rotary (Olfa) cutter and mat
plastic ruler and pencil
sewing thread
sewing machine

CUTTING
Do not forget to add seam allowances to each piece you cut.

1 Cut all the rectangles to 30 cm x 20 cm plus seam allowances. A rotary cutter will save time.

CONSTRUCTION
2 Lay out your quilt top (with six rectangles across and six down) and experiment with the arrangement. Join the top row together and then the next row. Continue in this way until you have six rows. Press. Mark them 1, 2, 3, 4, 5 and 6.

3 Join the six rows to complete the quilt top, following the order you have marked. Press.

4 Measure the width of the quilt top, measuring through the centre. Cut two strips of black fabric, each 9 cm plus seam allowances wide and as long as this measurement. Sew these to the top and bottom of the quilt top. Measure the length through the centre, including the top and bottom borders. Cut two strips of black fabric 9 cm wide plus seam allowances and as long as this measurement. Sew these to the sides of the quilt. Press the quilt top carefully.

5 Lay the backing fabric on a table, face down, and place the batting on top. Place the quilt top on top of that, face upwards. Baste or pin-baste through all thicknesses.

TYING
6 Using heavy crochet cotton, take a stitch at each corner and the centre of the rectangles. Tie the ends together twice securely, but don't pull too tightly. Trim the ends. For a more dramatic effect, use several strands of thread. Tie each one at these points. Trim off any excess backing and batting.

FINISHING
7 Measure the width of the quilt as before, to find the length of binding required. Cut two strips of black fabric, each 8 cm wide and as long as this measurement. Press the strips over double with wrong sides together. Sew the binding to the top and bottom of the quilt with right sides facing and raw edges even. Turn the binding to the wrong side and handsew into place. Repeat this process for binding the side edges.

STARS

Graceful hand-quilting is perfect for a simple pattern like the one in this quilt, designed and made by Dorothy Ison.

FABRIC SUGGESTIONS

A dark print and a medium print fabric have been used to define the stars on a plain cream background. Choose a third print for the border and then a plain fabric for the binding.

FINISHED SIZE

Quilt: 120 cm x 150 cm (approximately)
Block size: 30 cm x 30 cm

FABRIC QUANTITIES

1.5 m of 115 cm wide cream fabric
50 cm of 115 cm wide dark print fabric
50 cm of 115 cm wide medium print fabric
80 cm of 115 cm wide print fabric for the borders
60 cm of 115 cm wide plain fabric for binding
2.5 m of 115 cm wide fabric for backing, pieced to be 125 cm x 155 cm
125 cm x 155 cm batting

NOTIONS

cardboard or template plastic
pencil and ruler
safety pins, pins, needles and scissors
sewing thread and quilting thread
sewing machine

CUTTING

Do not forget to add seam allowances to each piece you cut.

1 Using the cardboard or plastic, trace and cut out the templates. For each block, cut four cream squares and one print square from template **a**; eight print triangles and eight cream triangles from template **b**.

In total, you will have six squares each in the two star prints, forty-eight cream squares, forty-eight triangles in each star print and ninety-six triangles in cream.

CONSTRUCTION

2 Chainsew the plain and print triangles together in pairs along one short side. Cut them apart. Press the seams to one side.

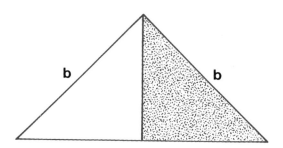

3 Join similar pairs along the long side to form a square, matching points and seams. Press.

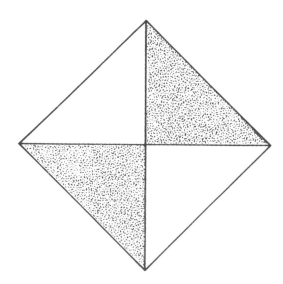

4 Taking the square just made, sew a cream square onto each coloured side. Press. Make two such strips, using the same print for each block.

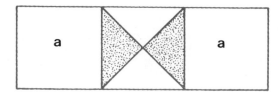

5 Sew two of the squares made in Step 3 to opposite sides of a matching print square. Press.

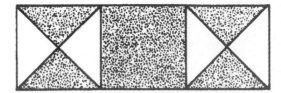

6 Join the pieces made in Steps 4 and 5 to make the complete block. Press. Make six blocks in each star print.

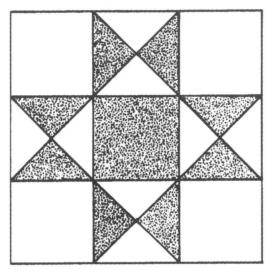

7 Join the blocks in rows of three blocks across, alternating the prints, to make the quilt top.

8 Measure the width of the quilt, measuring through the centre. Cut two strips of the border fabric to this length and 10 cm wide plus seam allowances. Sew these borders to the top and bottom of the quilt top. Measure the length of the quilt top, measuring through the centre and including the top and bottom borders. Cut two strips of the border fabric to this length and 10 cm wide plus seam allowances. Sew these to the sides of the quilt top. Press.

QUILTING

See the Pull Out Pattern Sheet at the back of the book for the quilting designs.

9 Using cardboard or template plastic, trace and cut out templates from the quilting patterns on the Pattern Sheet. Using the templates, mark the design onto the centre of each cream square and along the borders.

10 Lay the backing fabric, face down, on a table. Place the batting on top and the quilt top on top of that, face up. Baste or pin-baste all the layers together.

11 Quilt the marked designs on the cream squares and the borders. Hand-quilt along the seamlines and diagonally through the cream squares as shown.

12 Trim off any excess backing and batting.

FINISHING

13 Measure the quilt through the centre as before and cut binding fabric 10 cm wide plus seam allowances and the length of these measurements. Press the binding strips over double with wrong sides together. Place binding along the top and bottom edges of the quilt with raw edges even. Stitch the bindings in place. Repeat for the side bindings.

*Right: Detail of the
Stars quilt showing the
hand-quilting*

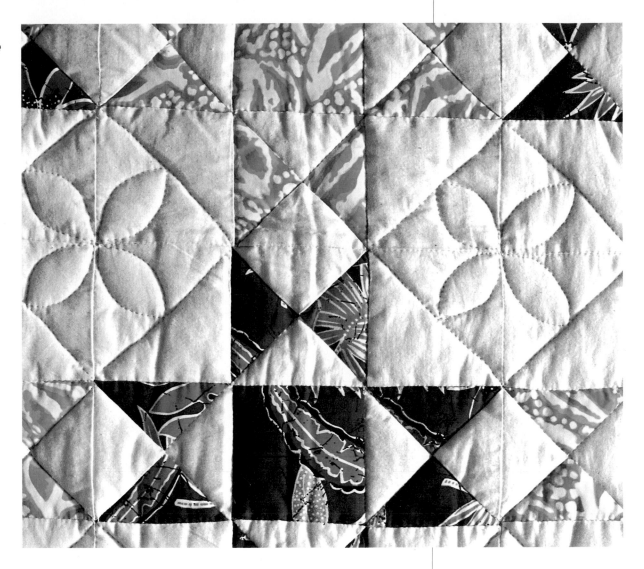

Templates

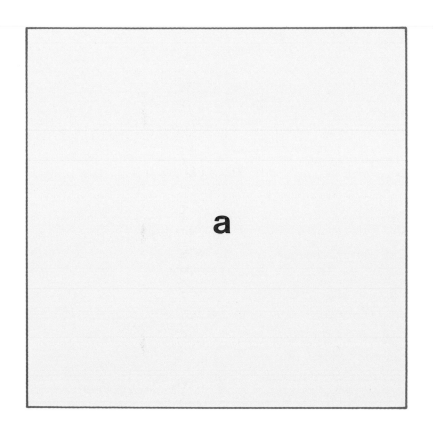

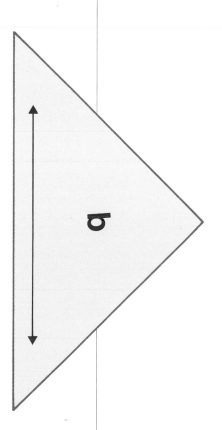

BASKET QUILT

Vicki Cordony is the proud owner of this fine example of a wonderful quilting tradition – the friendship quilt. Eight people contributed blocks to this hand-pieced and hand-quilted quilt.

FABRIC SUGGESTIONS

Various coloured cotton fabrics, utilising checks and stripes on a cream background have been used. The blocks are set on the diagonal. For the plain fabric, choose a homespun cloth and use it again for the backing.

FINISHED SIZE

Quilt: 150 cm x 176 cm
Block size: 18 cm
Total number of full blocks: 72
Total number of corner blocks: 4
Total number of border blocks: 22 half blocks

FABRIC QUANTITIES

2.5 m of 115 cm wide cotton background fabric
1.5 m of various 115 cm wide printed fabrics for the baskets
160 cm x 185 cm batting
3.2 m of cotton fabric (pieced to make 160 cm x 185 cm) for the backing
0.5 m of 115 cm wide cotton fabric for binding

NOTIONS

cardboard or template plastic
pencil and ruler
safety pins, pins, needles and scissors
sewing thread and quilting thread
sewing machine

CUTTING

Do not forget to add seam allowance to each piece you cut.

1 Cut templates **a**, **b**, **c**, **d**, and **e** from cardboard or template plastic. Lay the templates on the back of the fabric, matching grainlines on the fabric and templates. Draw around the templates with a sharp pencil. This pencil line will be the sewing line. Cut out with a 6 mm seam allowance.

2 *For each block:* Cut

template **a**	1 print
	1 plain background
template **b**	2 print
	2 plain background
template **c**	3 plain background

For the corner blocks: Cut

| template **d** | 4 plain background |

For the half blocks: Cut

| template **e** | 22 plain background |

For the handle, cut a bias strip 18 cm long and 3 cm wide from print fabric. Press in 6 mm on the raw edges on each side.

CONSTRUCTION

3 Appliqué a handle to one plain piece **a** along the dotted line with blind hem stitch. Sew the inner curve first. Press.

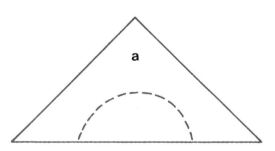

4 Join the handle triangle to the print triangle of the same size to form the handle square. Press.

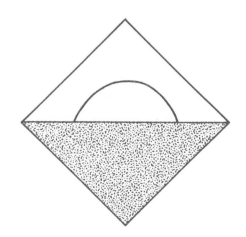

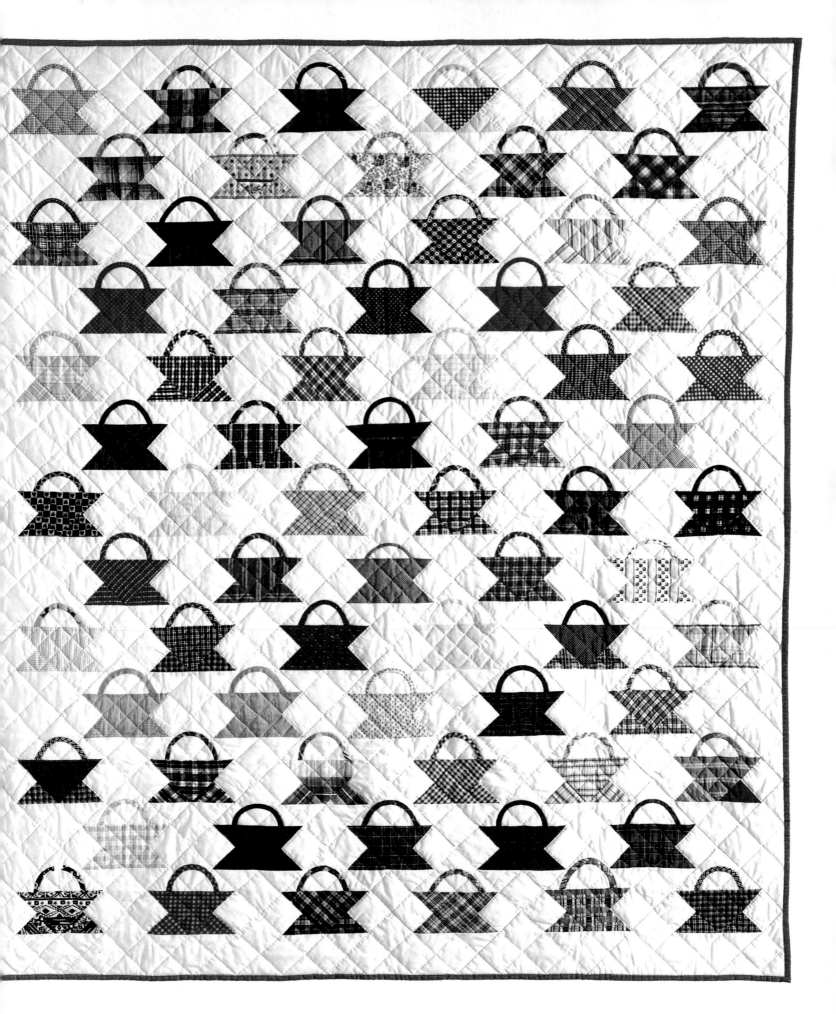

5 *To make Strip 1*: Join a print triangle **b** to a plain triangle **b** to make a square. Sew a plain square **c** to each side of the pieced square as marked. Press.

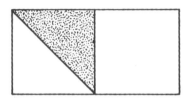

6 *To make Strip 2*: Join a print triangle **b** to a plain triangle **b** to make a square. Sew a plain square **c** to the print triangle side of this square as marked. Press.

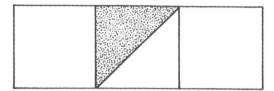

7 *To assemble the block*: Lay the handle square with the handle uppermost. Join Strip 2 to the lower right side of the handle square and

Below: A detail of the Basket Quilt showing the diagonal quilting

Strip 1 to the lower left side, including the short end of Strip 2. Press.

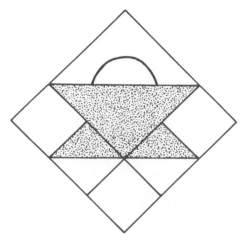

8 Lay out the 72 blocks in a pleasing colour arrangement. Join them together, adding in the corner blocks and half blocks. Press.

QUILTING

9 Lay the backing fabric face down on a table, with the batting on top. Place the pieced quilt top on top of that, face up. Smooth out any wrinkles. Baste or pin-baste through all the layers.

10 Hand-quilt the printed fabric into 2.5 cm squares. The plain fabric is quilted along the seamlines.

11 Trim off any excess backing and batting.

FINISHING

12 *For the binding*: Cut the fabric into 7 cm wide strips. Join strips together to achieve the desired lengths to bind the sides first and then the top and bottom, measuring through the centre of the quilt lengthways and widthways to determine the lengths required. Fold the strips over double with wrong sides together and raw edges even. Press. Sew the binding to the front of the quilt, with raw edges matching, and turn the pressed edge to the wrong side. Slipstitch the pressed edge to the back of the quilt.

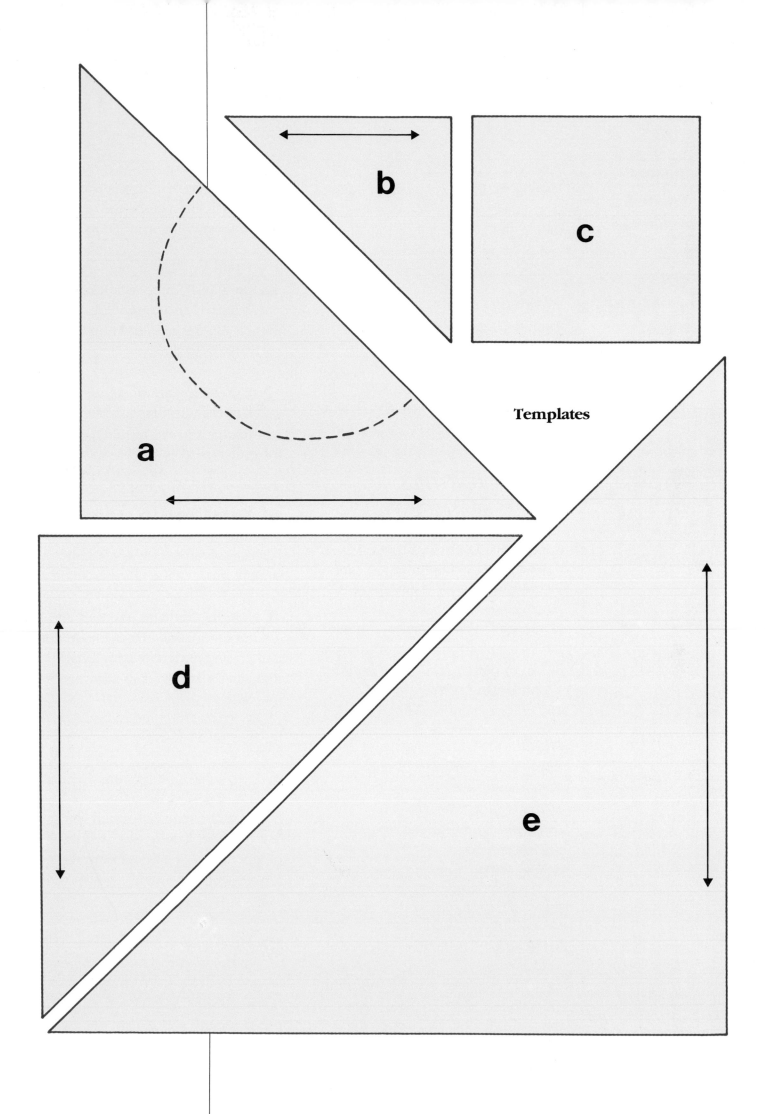

Templates

TRIANGLE WALL QUILT

Colour is crucial in this dazzling quilt, designed and made by Beryl Hodges. This quilt has been machine-pieced and machine-quilted.

FABRIC SUGGESTIONS

Having decided on your four colours to contrast with the black, choose four toning shades of each one. You can use both print and plain cotton dress fabrics as long as the tones are right.

FINISHED SIZE

Quilt: 147 cm x 105 cm (approximately)
Block size: 10 cm triangle
Total number of full blocks: 207 (103 black and 104 coloured)
Total half blocks: 18 (10 black and 8 coloured)

FABRIC QUANTITIES

All fabrics are 115 cm wide
1 m black fabric for the triangles
1.3 m black fabric for the second border and bindings
20 cm each of four shades of blue
20 cm each of four shades of pink
20 cm each of four shades of green
20 cm each of four shades of purple
30 cm of border fabric (first border)
1.5 m backing fabric
150 cm x 110 cm wadding

NOTIONS

cardboard or template plastic
pencil and ruler
rotary (Olfa) cutter and mat
safety pins, pins, needles and scissors
sewing machine
sewing thread

CUTTING

Do not forget to add seam allowances to each piece you cut.

1 Cut templates **a** and **b** from firm cardboard or template plastic. Lay the templates on the back of the fabric, with base of triangle along grainline of fabric. Trace around the template using a firm, sharp pencil. This pencil line will be the sewing line. Cut out with seam allowances.

2 Using template **a**, cut: one hundred and three black triangles and one hundred and four coloured triangles in the required numbers for each shade as shown.

3 Using template **b**, cut: ten black half triangles, and eight coloured half triangles in the required numbers for each shade as shown.

CONSTRUCTION

4 Lay out the black and coloured triangles and half triangles in the correct colour layout, placing the straight grain of the fabric horizontally.

5 Join the triangles together into nine horizontal rows, beginning and ending each row with a half triangle. Press the seam allowances to one side.

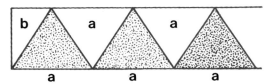

6 Sew the nine horizontal rows together, taking care that the points match exactly, to form the quilt top. Press the seam allowances to one side.

7 Measure down through the centre of the quilt top to determine its length. Cut two strips of the coloured border fabric the same length as this measurement and 2.5 cm plus seam allowances wide. Join strips if neces-

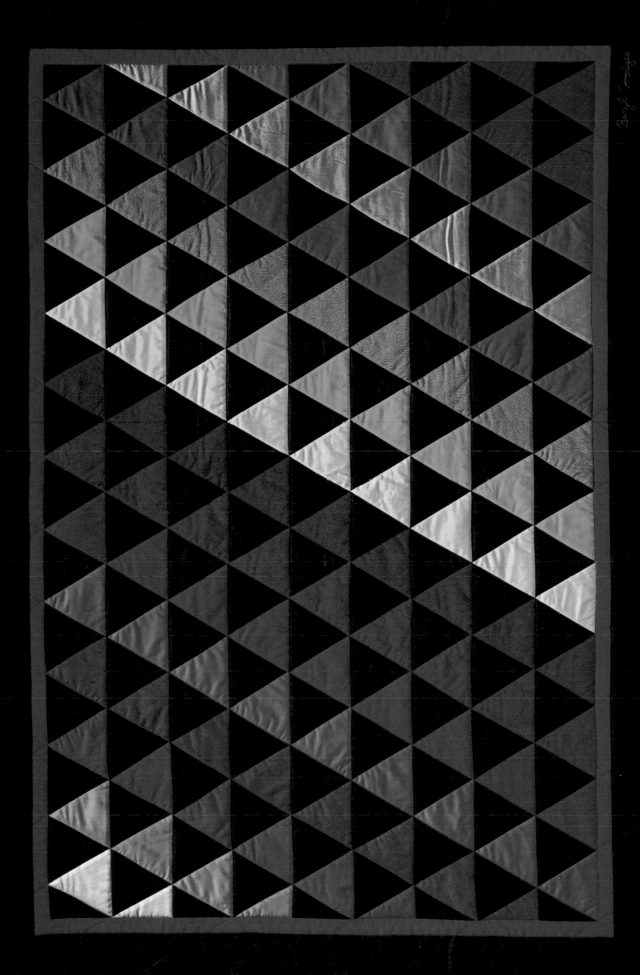

sary to achieve the length required. Sew these strips to each short side of the quilt top, taking care to sew exactly at the points of the triangles.

8 Measure across through the centre of the quilt top, including the border strips, to find the width. Cut two strips of coloured border fabric as for the side borders and attach in the same way.

9 Repeat steps 7 and 8 for the black border, cutting the strips 10 cm wide plus seam allowances. Press the quilt top carefully.

10 Assemble the layers of the quilt on a table with the backing facing down, the wadding in between and the quilt top facing upwards. Baste with big stitches or pin-baste through all thicknesses to secure the three layers of the quilt together.

QUILTING

11 Machine-quilt in the seamlines of the triangles and borders, taking the quilting stitching through the borders all the way to the edges.

FINISHING

12 Trim off excess wadding and backing. Cut two lengths of 8 cm wide black binding for the quilt sides and two lengths for the quilt top and bottom. Measure through the centres, as before, to determine the lengths. Press the strips over double with wrong sides together. Place the binding on the right side of the quilt with raw edges even. Stitch. Turn the binding to the wrong side and slipstitch into place.

13 Sew a sleeve along the top of the quilt back, so that a light batten can be threaded through for hanging. Sign and date your quilt.

Right: Detail of the Triangle Wall Quilt showing the borders and the diagonal quilting

CARE OF QUILTS

Look after your quilt and it will last long enough to become a family heirloom. The enemies are dust, light, humidity and insects. Good housekeeping will help to preserve your quilt and protect it from damage.

Cotton quilts should be washed in your washing machine on a gentle cycle, in warm water, and dried flat in the shade. Quilts should not be exposed to strong light. If you need to store a quilt for long periods, take it out regularly for airing every six months and then fold it in a different way before putting it back into store.

The correct way to fold a quilt when it is not in use, is to fold it with the right side outwards. Then put it into a bag made of well-washed cotton fabric along with rolls of acid-free tissue paper, tucked into the folds. Never store a quilt in a plastic bag as this traps humidity in the enclosed air and causes discoloration. The cotton bag, with the quilt inside, can be put into a cardboard box with mothballs outside the bag to discourage insects.

Most important of all, your quilt was made to be enjoyed for its usefulness and admired for its beauty.

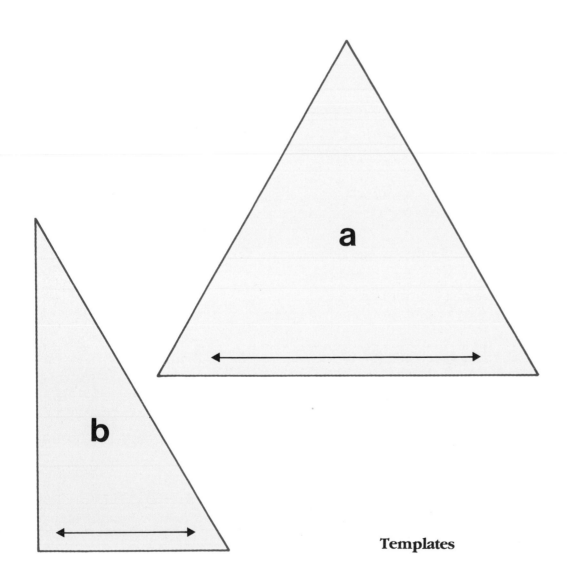

Templates

FLYING GEESE

In this traditional quilt, designed and made by Ann Crafter, the pattern works in parallel lines of triangles along the length of the quilt. It is not difficult to imagine that the triangles are in fact geese flying in formation, with outstretched wings.

FABRIC SUGGESTIONS

The 'sky' triangles are often white or cream and the 'geese' are either in a combination of toning colours and fabrics (as in this quilt) or in a single contrasting colour. For our quilt we have chosen six different fabrics for the 'geese' – two light, two medium and two dark. The interesting striped sashes are not pieced but are in fact cut from a striped fabric which gives the effect of being pieced from a number of different stripes.

This quilt is machine-pieced and machine-quilted.

Seam allowances of 6 mm have been included.

FINISHED SIZE

Quilt: 124 cm x 103 cm (approximately)
Block size: 18 cm x 9 cm
Total number of full blocks: 30

FABRIC QUANTITIES

6 different scrap fabrics for the geese
All the following fabrics are 115 cm wide:
80 cm light colour for the background
    paisley striped fabric for the sashes
50 cm dark plain colour for border
40 cm contrasting plain fabric for
    binding
130 cm x 115 m plain fabric for
backing
130 cm x 110 cm batting

NOTIONS

cardboard or template plastic
pencil and ruler
rotary (Olfa) cutter and mat
safety pins, pins, needles and scissors
sewing thread
sewing machine

CUTTING

1 Cut 11.5 cm wide strips from the six colours of scrap fabric and 11.5 cm strips from the light background colour. Cut these into 11.5 cm lengths to make squares.

2 Cut four sashes from the striped fabric to be approximately 9 cm wide and 91.5 cm long.

CONSTRUCTION

3 Place one background square and one print square together with right sides facing and draw a line diagonally from one corner to the other. Sew a line of stitching 6 mm on either side of this line.

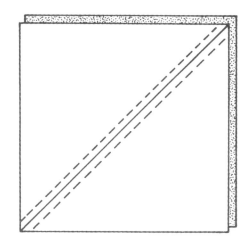

4 Cut along the pencil line, open out the fabric and you will have

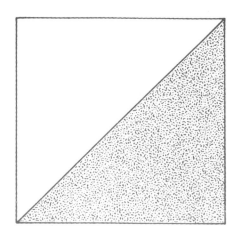

two new squares half 'goose' and half background. Sew the 'goose' sides of the squares together, matching print fabrics, to make a rectangular block. Press. Make five of these blocks in each print fabric, making a total of thirty blocks.

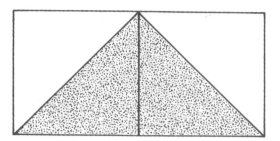

5 Lay the rectangles out in three rows of ten so that you can judge the arrangement of colours and prints. Sew them into three strips. Make sure that the geese are 'flying' in the same direction across the quilt when the strips are laid next to each other. Press.

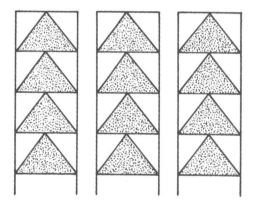

6 Join the three 'geese' strips with striped sashes in between and on the outside, making sure the rectangles are in line. The sashes on the outside form the inner border. Measure across the centre to find the width of the quilt top. Cut two sashes to this width. Sew them to the top and bottom of the quilt top. Press.

7 Measure down the centre of the quilt to find the full length. Cut two outside borders from the plain, dark fabric of this length and 9.5 cm wide. Sew them to the sides of the quilt. Measure through the centre of the quilt top, including the borders just attached, to find the full width. Cut two outer borders to this length and 9.5 cm wide. Sew them to the top and bottom of the quilt top. Press the quilt top carefully.

8 Cut the backing fabric to size and place it right side down. If you can fit it on a table, sticky tape it to the table to stop it from slipping. Place the batting over the backing and the pieced quilt top over this, with the right side up. Smooth out any wrinkles and, using safety pins, pin the three layers together all over the quilt.

QUILTING

9 Starting in the middle of the quilt (using a walking foot, if you have one) stitch around the 'geese' triangles first.

TIP

It's a good idea to do the quilting in zigzag lines, working down only one side of each 'goose' from top to bottom, and then stitching the other side from top to bottom. This means you can work in continuous rows without too much starting and stopping in your sewing.

10 Stitch across the striped borders with parallel rows of stitching, approximately 3 cm apart. Take care to mark this out first so you end up with even rows at the corners. The plain dark border and the sashes are quilted in with joined ovals, the pattern for which is given opposite. Trace the design and make a template for your stitching. Transfer the design to your fabric, using a silver pencil or a water-soluble pencil. Trim off any excess backing and batting.

FINISHING

11 Measure through the centre of the quilt lengthways and crossways as before to determine the lengths of the binding strips. Cut the binding to be 8 cm wide. Press the binding strips over double with wrong sides together. Stitch the binding to the right side of the quilt with raw edges even. Turn the binding to the wrong side of the quilt and handsew it into place.

Quilting design

Above: Detail of quilt showing the border, sashes and quilting

GARDEN PATH

Lynette McKinley, designer and quiltmaker, chose a lush floral print to combine with a strong geometric pattern. The quilt has been machine-pieced and machine-quilted.

FABRIC SUGGESTIONS

For added interest, the floral design works in striped panels and the triangular template **c** has been cut from different parts of the stripe. This process does involve a lot of wastage so you will need to be generous when buying fabric. The quilt, which has been made using six each of two blocks, can be enlarged by adding more blocks.

6 mm seam allowances are included.

FINISHED SIZE

Quilt: 119 cm x 150 cm (approximately)
Block size: 31 cm square
Total number of full blocks: 12

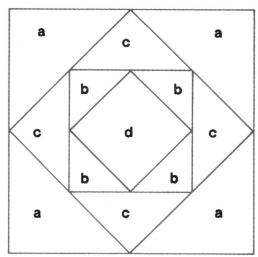

Block 1

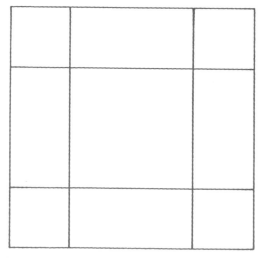

Block 2

FABRIC QUANTITIES

1 m (approximately) of striped floral fabric
60 cm blue fabric for small triangles
70 cm cream fabric for large triangles and blocks
20 cm red print fabric
40 cm plain red fabric
1.6 m striped fabric for borders
3.1 m of 115 cm wide backing fabric pieced to make 125 cm x 155 cm (if you have a crossways seam in the backing you can reduce this to 2.5 m)
125 cm x 155 cm batting

NOTIONS

template plastic
pencil and ruler
rotary (Olfa) cutter and mat
safety pins, pins, needles and scissors
sewing thread and quilting thread
(This quilt has been quilted with invisible thread.)
sewing machine

CUTTING

See the Pull Out Pattern Sheet for the templates.

For Block 1:

1 Cut the four templates out of transparent plastic so you can plan the placement of the fabric pattern. Cut template **d** six times out of the centre roses, placing each one the same way on the fabric.

2 Fold the blue fabric in half and then fold it again so you have four layers. After straightening the edge and

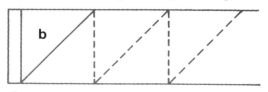

↑ *Cut off selvage*

cutting off the selvages, cut a strip 10 cm wide using scissors or, preferably, a rotary cutter and plastic ruler. Lay template **b** along the strip as shown and cut out twenty-four triangles.

3 The next triangles, **c**, are cut individually from the striped material. Lay the see-through template down over a particular stripe and cut four triangles the same from each section for each of the six blocks.

4 From the cream fabric, cut two strips across the width of the fabric each 17 cm wide. Cut twenty-four triangles from the cream fabric using template **a**.

For Block 2:

5 Folding the fabric into four as for the blue fabric, cut two 9 cm wide strips across the width of the floral fabric. Cut one 16.5 cm wide strip across the plain cream fabric. Cut two 9 cm wide and one 16.5 cm wide strips from the plain red fabric.

CONSTRUCTION

6 *To make Block 1*: Sew the long side of a blue triangle to all four sides of the small floral square cut

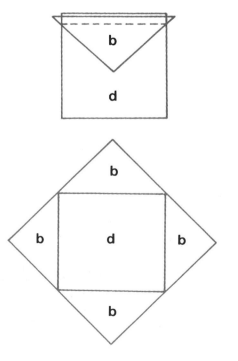

from template **d**. They should extend beyond the corners of the square to enable the next triangle to go on without losing the point of the square.

7 Join four striped triangles to the sides of the square and then sew on four plain cream triangles. Make five more of these blocks. Press all the blocks carefully.

8 *To make Block 2*: Join the two floral strips across their width with the one 16.5 cm wide plain red strip in between.

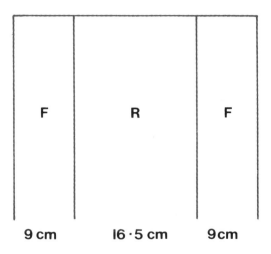

9 Press the seams to one side and cut the joined strip into strips 9 cm wide.

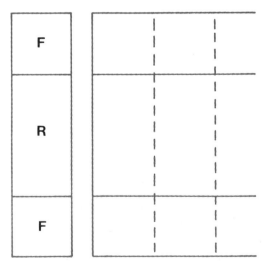

10 Join a 9 cm wide strip of plain red to each long side of the 16.5 cm plain cream strip. Press the seams to one side and cut into strips

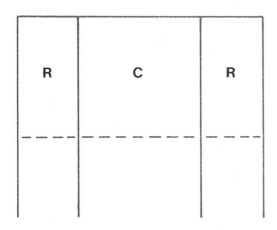

R	C	R

16.5 cm wide. Piece two strips with the floral squares on both ends to two opposite sides of the plain red and cream strip. Make five more of these blocks. Press all blocks carefully.

F	R	F
R	C	R
F	R	F

11 Piece the quilt together, alternating blocks and matching corners carefully. Sew in rows, first Block 1, then Block 2, then Block 1. In the second row, join Block 2, Block 1, then Block 2. For the third row, join Block 1, then Block 2, then Block 1 and so on. Continue until the quilt is finished.

12 Measure the width of the quilt through the centre. Cut the border from the striped fabric to this length, using whatever width best complements your stripes. Join the borders to the top and bottom of the quilt. Press. Repeat for the border on the sides of the quilt.

QUILTING

13 Place the backing fabric face down on a table and sticky tape it to the table to prevent it slipping. Place the batting on top and then the pieced quilt top on top of that, face up. Carefully smooth out all the wrinkles. Using large safety pins and starting in the middle of the quilt, pin all three layers together. Machine-quilt, or hand-quilt if you prefer, the complete top with criss-crossing diagonal rows of stitching, about 6 cm apart. Trim off any excess backing and batting.

FINISHING

14 Cut 8 cm wide strips from the plain red fabric for the binding. Measure across the centre of the quilt to find the length and width to calculate the length of binding required. The edges of a quilt are sometimes stretched and it may ripple along the edges and not sit straight, making accurate measurement a problem. Fold the binding strip over double with wrong sides together and raw edges matching. Sew to the top and bottom edges of the quilt, stretching the binding to fit along the edges. Sew the rest to both sides of the quilt. Turn to the back of the quilt and handsew in place.

KEY

R = RED
C = CREAM
F = FLORAL

Below: Detail of the Garden Path quilt showing the criss-crossing machine quillting

PATCHWORK NURSERY QUILT

Kate McEwen made this nursery quilt using four different but harmonising patterns in dress-weight cotton. Here we include two options for this pretty nursery quilt design. This very easy-to-sew quilt is machine-pieced and machine-quilted.

FABRIC SUGGESTIONS

Mix patterns and plain fabrics as well as colours, picking up some of those fabrics in some frilled curtains.

FINISHED SIZE

Quilt: 88 cm x 120 cm
Block size: 14 cm x 14 cm
Total number of blocks: 24

FABRIC QUANTITIES

30 cm of 115 cm wide cream cotton fabric

1.5 m of 115 cm wide cotton fabric for strips, binding and backing

70 cm each of two other 115 cm wide fabrics

88 cm x 120 cm batting

NOTIONS

pencil and ruler
rotary (Olfa) cutter and mat
safety pins, pins and scissors
sewing machine

CUTTING

1 cm seam allowances are included in the cutting instructions

1 Cut 4.4 m of 6 cm wide strips in each of the four fabrics. Join strips to achieve the necessary length.

CONSTRUCTION

2 Join the four strips together lengthways in whatever colour arrangement you like, forming a strip approximately 18 cm wide. Press the seams to one side.

3 Cut the strip into 18 cm lengths, to make twenty-four 18 cm squares.

4 Lay the squares out, in four rows of six, taking care to alternate the direction of the seams in the blocks as shown. Sew the squares into rows, then join the rows to form the quilt top. Press.

5 Measure the width of the quilt, measuring through the centre. Cut two strips of the inner border fabric to this length and 6 cm wide. Sew these to the top and bottom of the quilt top. Measure the length of the quilt top, including the top and bottom borders. Cut two strips of the inner border fabric to this length and 6 cm wide. Sew these to the sides of the quilt.

6 Repeat the process in Step 5 for the outer border, cutting the fabric 10 cm wide.

QUILTING

7 Place the backing fabric face down on a table. Place the batting on top and the quilt top on top of that, facing upwards. Pin-baste the three layers together.

8 Machine-quilt around all the blocks and borders in the seamlines.

FINISHING

9 Measure the width of the quilt as before and cut the binding fabric 6 cm wide to this length. Fold the binding strip over double lengthways, with wrong sides together. Sew the binding to the right side of the top and bottom of the quilt with raw edges even. Repeat for the side bindings.

Left: A delightful
addition to any nursery
Below left: Try a slightly
different arrangement
of colours and strips
Below: Keep your baby
cosy and warm with a
special quilt

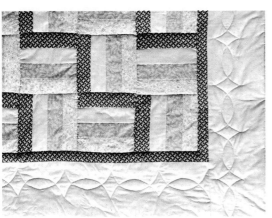

99

Lily of the Valley
flowers and leaves

Cornelli Work Pattern

Tablecloth motifs
For Shadow Work

Bow for Camisole

Bow in centre
under mongram

Bows for Panties
For Shadow Work

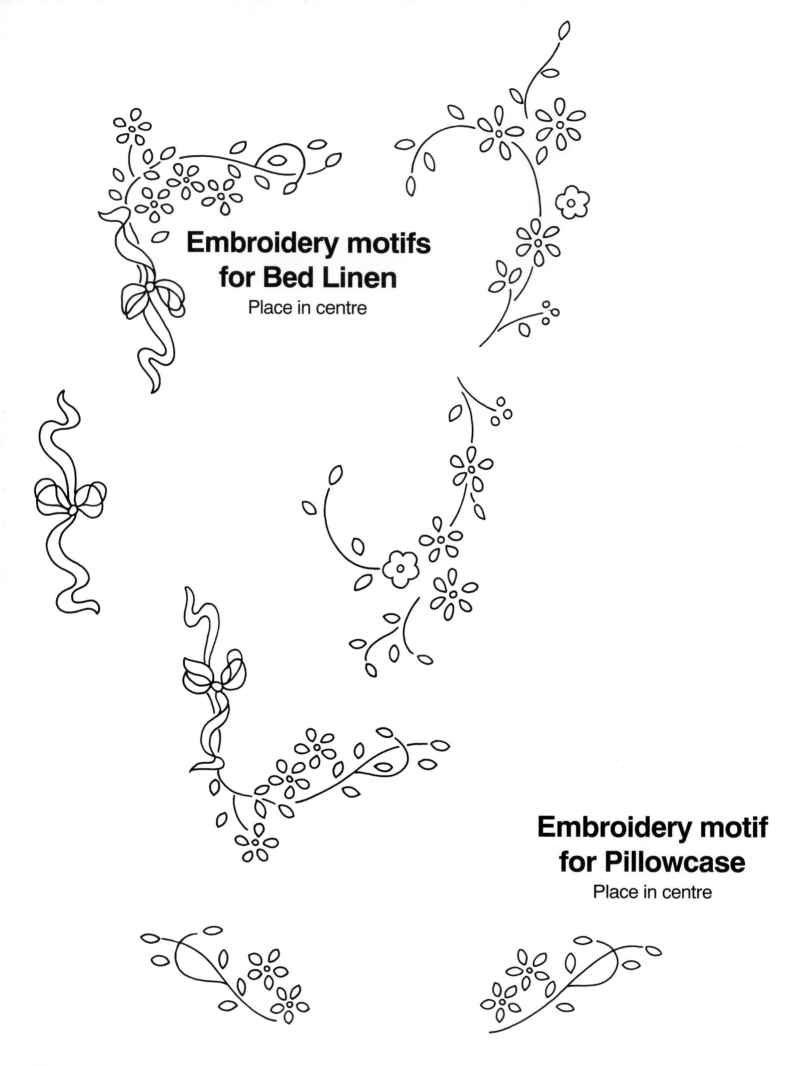

Embroidery motifs
for Bed Linen
Place in centre

Embroidery motif
for Pillowcase
Place in centre

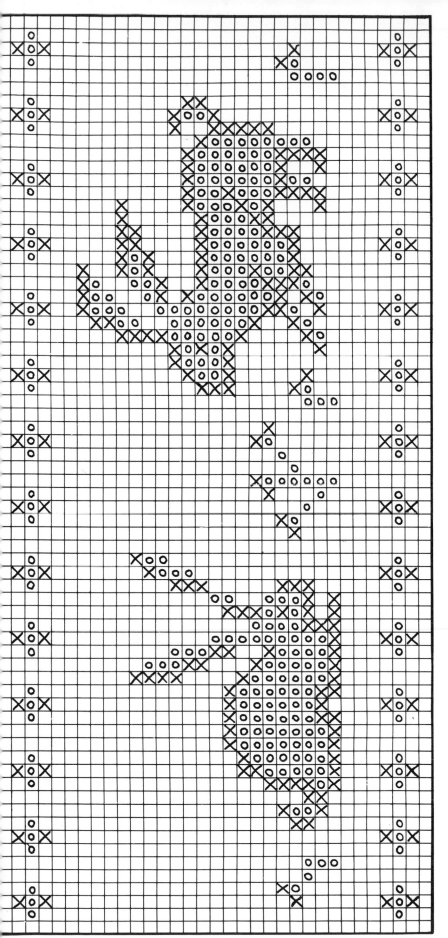

Cross Stitch Graph
for Rabbits

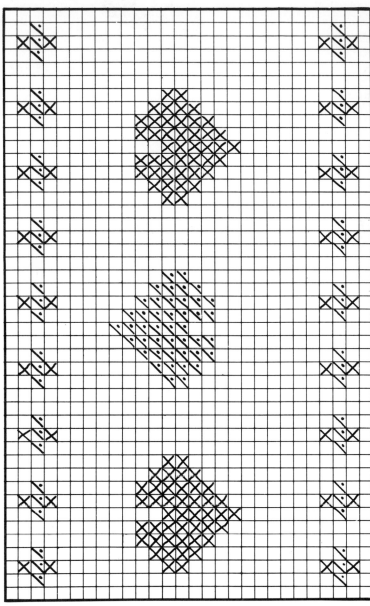

Cross Stitch Graph
for Hearts

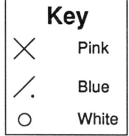

Key

✕	Pink
╱.	Blue
○	White

Nasturtium and Border
Stencil Design

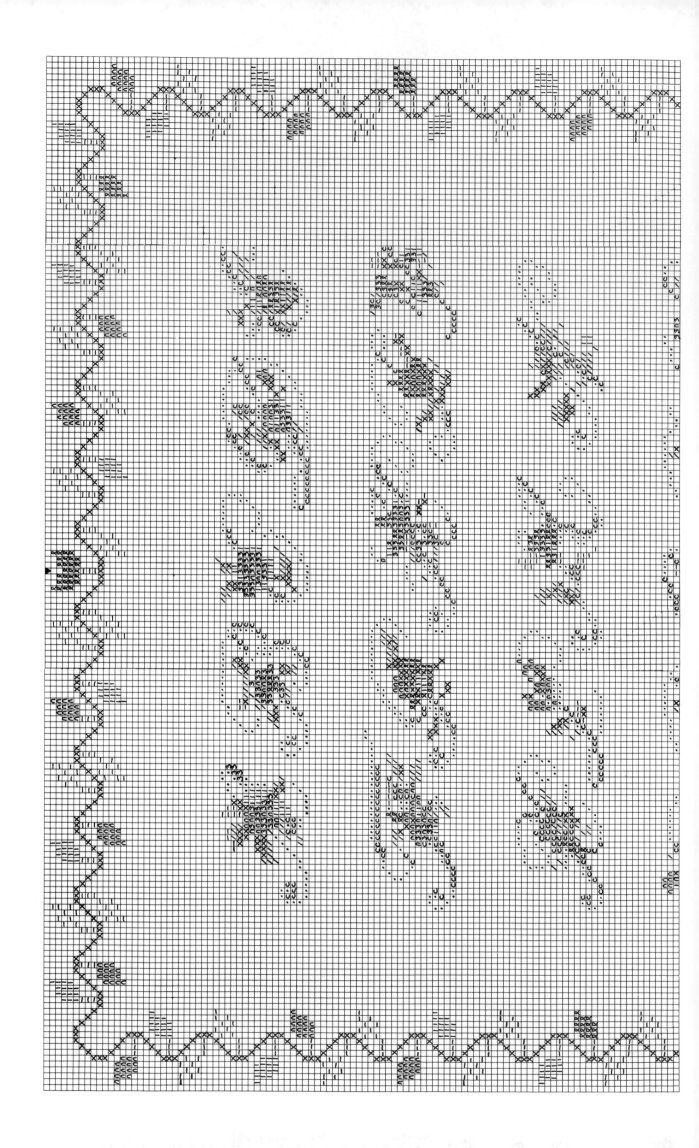

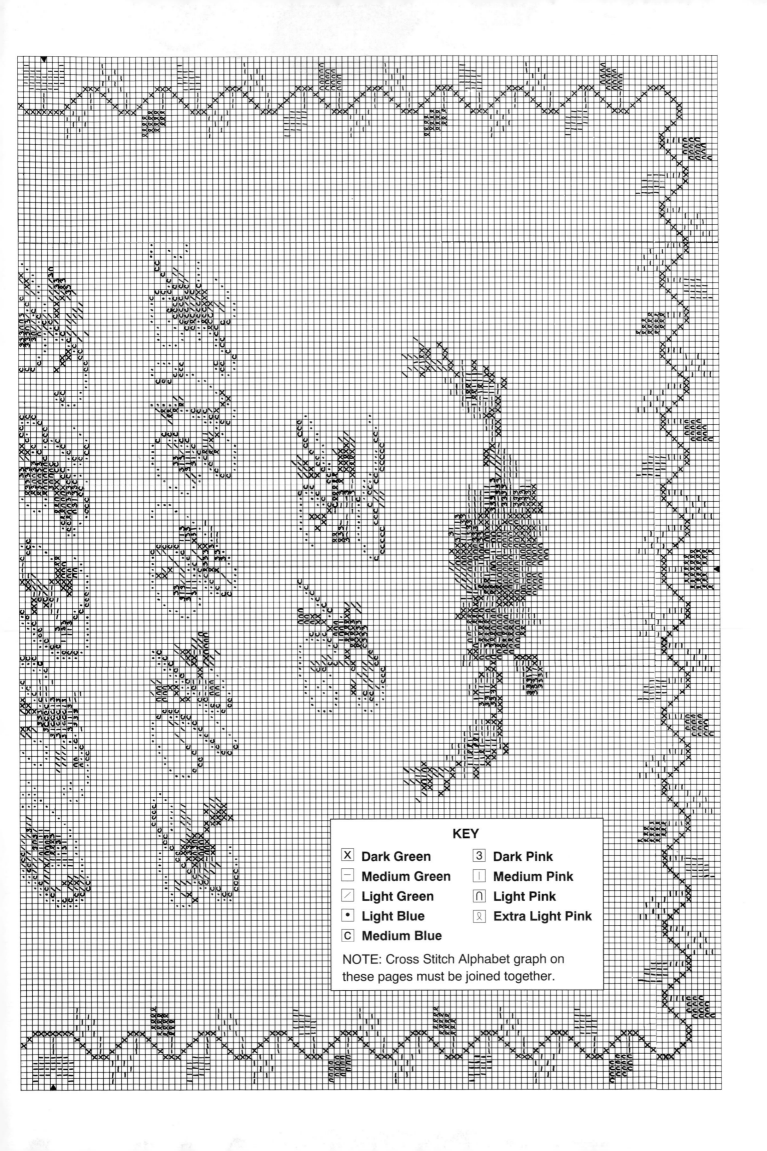

KEY

X	Dark Green	3	Dark Pink
−	Medium Green	I	Medium Pink
∕	Light Green	∩	Light Pink
•	Light Blue	ℓ	Extra Light Pink
C	Medium Blue		

NOTE: Cross Stitch Alphabet graph on these pages must be joined together.

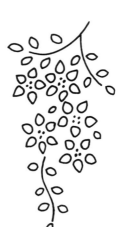

Embroidery motifs
for Boudoir Cushion

Place at random
across fabric

Single Irish Chain Quilt
Main Quilting Pattern

Single Irish Chain Quilt
Clover Leaf Pattern

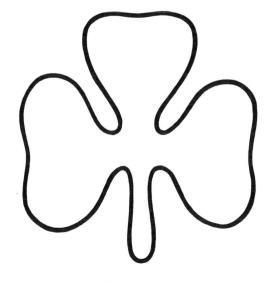

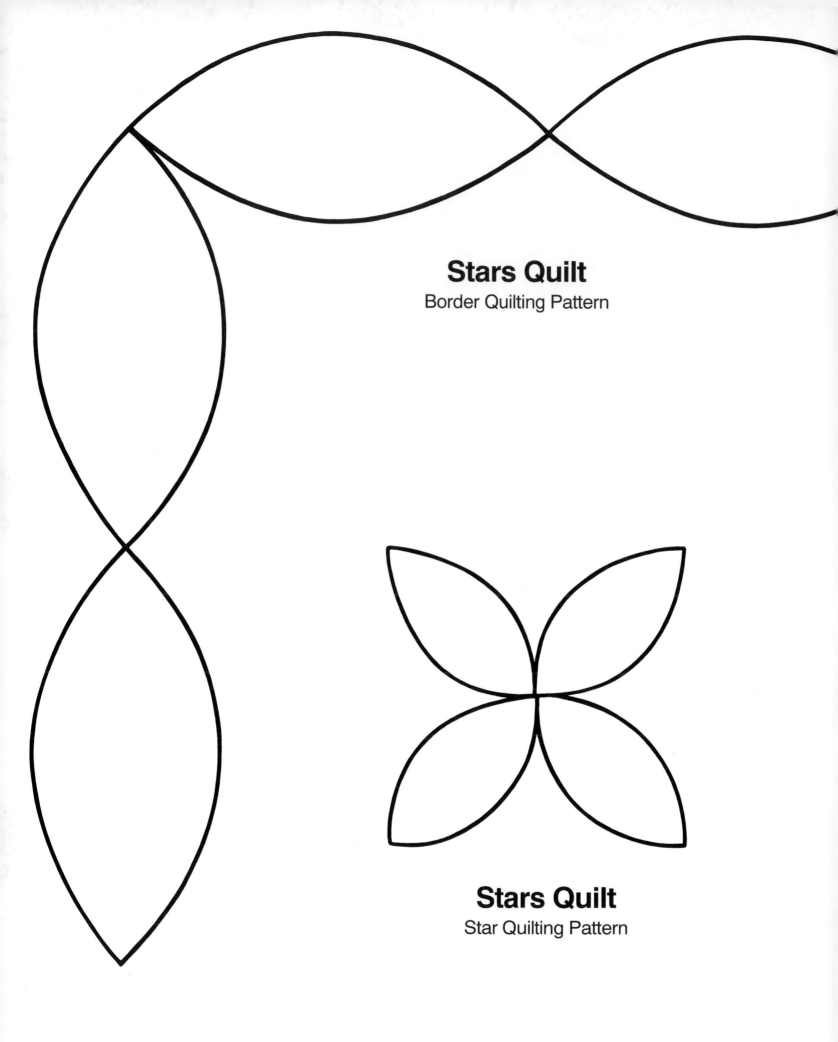

Stars Quilt

Border Quilting Pattern

Stars Quilt

Star Quilting Pattern

Garden Path Quilt

Templates

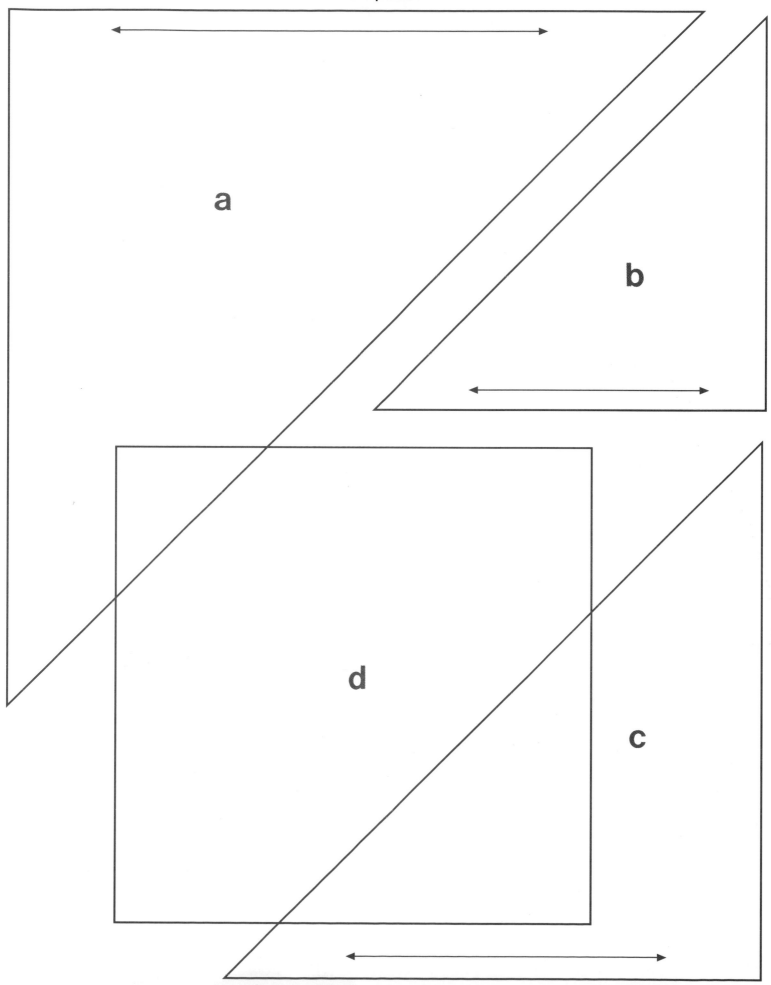

Monogram Alphabet

A B C D E

F G H I J

K L M N

O P Q R

S T U V W

X Y Z